Folk We've Met

The Story of Munlochy Animal Aid

Iona Nicol MBE

Bassman Books

Published by Bassman Books, Burnside Cottage,
Newhall, Balblair, Dingwall, IV7 8LT

First published in 2019

A catalogue record for this book is available from the
British Library

ISBN 978-0-9956440-2-1

Printed by Big Sky, The Press Building,
305 The Park, Findhorn, Forres, IV36 3TE

Layout and design by Russell Turner
www.russellturner.org
Set in Palatino 11/13pt

MIX
Paper from
responsible sources
FSC® C020891

Dedication

"We could write a book!" How many times we have talked about this but just never seemed to get the words onto paper. So many stories to tell and now, sadly, my mother is no longer with us. Her memory was much better than mine. Opening a rescue centre seemed such a good idea, but giving up your life to it is a different story - believe me!

This book is a tribute to my mother and father, Margaret and Alec, acknowledging their remarkable strength and courage, helping us achieve something very special.

Graham and Iona on their wedding day getting the blessing of Flash.

Folk We've Met

Dogs and puppies
Kittens and cats
Hedgehogs and squirrels
Ferrets and rats.

There's a deer in the garden
A duck in the bath
While the sheep and the ponies
Graze the croft path.

Iguanas and otters
We've had them all
While up overhead
Our seagulls call.

Tiger is a wildcat
(Scruffy's best friend)
But the call of the wild
Won out in the end.

While Lucky and Lady
Enjoy piggy wallows
Their humble abode
Is 'home' to our swallows.

Lots of pleasure
(and some pain)
But we'd do it all over
Again and again.

Iona Nicol

Cathy at the end of her sponsored bike ride from Lands End to John O'Groats.

Foreword

I had only been working at the veterinary surgery in Conon Bridge for a few days when Hamish Sutherland, then the senior partner, called me into his consulting room to introduce me to Iona who, with her parents and sister, ran the animal rescue home at Munlochy. This was in 1991, and was the start of a long and interesting, sometimes very challenging, experience as Munlochy Animal Aid takes in a wide variety of species, both wild and domestic. They could come up with an even wider variety of problems, many of which we hadn't been told about at college.

An impressive number of pets which passed through the surgery were 'from Munlochy' and nearly all of them had become well-established family members with delighted owners. I sometimes felt that Iona must supply at least half the pets in the Highlands. I myself have had quite a few animals from MAA, mainly cats and dogs, but also an iguana (for 19 years) and an old horse who came to spend the last years of her life with me. Of the current population at home, both dogs and two of the cats are former MAA residents. My saluki lurcher, Ajax, was born there.

MAA is a happy, friendly environment where all the animals are treated as individuals by Iona and her husband Graham, and all the dedicated staff and volunteers who work tirelessly to attend to their needs.

This is the story of their first 40 years. I don't know what we would do without them.

Catherine Macquarrie BVMS MRCVS

Contents

Chapter 1

In the Beginning

I have spent my entire life surrounded by animals. My mother and father both adored cats and would always feed any that turned up: my granny was the same. Her husband died when my father was just fourteen, leaving her with six children to bring up on a wee croft. There was very little money but she always managed to feed any cat that arrived.

I cannot remember much about my early years except the night when I was two years old and my father arrived with a German Shepherd dog. We were at the kitchen table having our meal and Dad was late, and he was never late. Then he arrived and came in the front door, which was unheard of. With him was a huge young adult male German Shepherd dog. I remember, vividly, taking my plate and holding it in front of the dog for him to eat from.

My mother told Dad that she was not having that big dog in the house, what with Iona being so small. Of course, the next morning my mother was madly in love with Flash, as we all were. He was a fantastic dog and he really was the centre of our family. He would wake us up in the morning by nibbling our toes and when it snowed, he would pull the sledge, my older sister, Alexis, running ahead and me on the sledge until I was thrown off into the ditch. Even that never put me off and we had such a lot of fun with that dog. Flash got along with all the many cats and kittens. He would go every day to visit with Granny and never used a lead since the roads were very quiet in those days. He lived to be a ripe old age and we were all heartbroken at the loss of that very special dog.

In those days, it was almost unheard of to have a cat neutered so there were always kittens looking for homes. People could not give kittens away because everybody had all the cats they wanted and, fortunately, today it is much harder to find a kitten. Therefore, unwanted kittens, and even puppies, were often drowned. We heard of people who did not want their dog any more, so took it outside and shot it. There was no kennel up in the Highlands where people could take an unwanted dog.

There was a different attitude towards dogs anyway. They were mainly guard dogs, sheep dogs or other working dogs but we rarely saw people like us with seven dogs in their house just for the pleasure of their company. People did not seem to enjoy their dogs so much in those days.

Rescuing animals has been a way of life for me. Mum and Dad would take on dogs that they heard needed help and care, not necessarily to keep them but sometimes they stayed for years. There was one particular Corgi that we took in for a holiday and then the stay became a bit longer and a bit longer, until it got so that my father did not want it to go back. When the owners announced that they were moving, my father decided the dog could not cope with that and was overjoyed when it was decided that we should keep the dog. Mum and Dad adored animals. In fact, I think Mum liked dogs and cats more than she liked children and she was certainly kinder to them than to me and my sister! So it was that, one by one, the family of cats and dogs increased.

At one particular time I had a wee doggie and when he died, very suddenly, I was so distressed that Mum suggested we went to the dog pound in Inverness to get another dog. My mother remembered seeing a horrid old dog pound where strays were put into a big shed and you can imagine the fighting that went on, but by this time it was a new pound. This new one was an eye-opener for me because I could not believe that dogs were kept in those conditions. There was no heating, and winters were really cold then, and nothing but pallets to lie on. The pound would flood at high tide and no matter whether they were old dogs or puppies they had to stand in the water. I found it shocking and I can still visualise it. I could not believe that dogs were kept in such horrible conditions. Whether the dog was a six-week-old puppy or a sixteen-year-old dog, they all got the same awful food to eat. Eventually, Mum and I were going backwards and forwards to both Inverness and Dingwall dog pounds with food for the animals and it was exhausting until two friends, Muriel and Sandy, took on some of the Dingwall feeding.

We rescued this little black dog from the pound. He was a cross-breed, but a cross between what I have no idea: we called him Tammy. I so wanted to do something about the conditions into which these animals were put but I was working then at a firm in Inverness so I could not do much about it. Then one day Mum rang me at work to say she had heard something on the radio about someone who was setting up a rescue charity locally and were in need of volunteers. My family provided some of the necessary items that were needed to run the charity and then I gave up work to help. However, there were still so many dogs being destroyed that we realised it would be better if we were doing some of this rescuing ourselves.

Dad, who was a builder, set up one of the outbuildings for us to use as a kennel. We had runs down both sides and he put in a massive heater so the dogs could be warm no matter what the weather. Each dog had a comfy second-hand sofa for a bed and, since they came from the pound, they must have thought it was heaven. As we became known, some people came to us when they were looking for a dog but more and more people started approaching us to take dogs they could not keep, or did not want to keep any more. We began to realise just how much of a gap we had filled and the whole thing started to take off.

The council then started making us buy the dogs from the pound and in the 1980s £21 for a stray was a lot of money, especially since they were only going to put them down after seven days. I went into the pound one day and the dog warden pointed out four dogs and said those four were all being put down the next day unless we took them at £21 each. He knew that I would find the money. Both Mum and Granny kept hens and we sold eggs to the Egg Marketing Board to make extra money but money was always an issue.

We offered to help the pound by putting in heating and doing anything else they needed done in order to make it more comfortable for the dogs. We were making it very clear that we did not like the way that it was. They surprised us then by banning us from taking any more dogs. The council said they could not understand what we were doing with all these dogs! This state of affairs came to the attention of a journalist who made public the fact that he thought it was ludicrous that they were killing dogs when we were offering them a chance at life.

We had a much better relationship with the pound in Dingwall than in Inverness. Dingwall accepted help from us up to the point where they would let us access it whenever we wanted. So, by now we needed more space and mum and I extended into another one of Dad's sheds. We included a wee kitchen and four more pens. These were not very big, but if we got a poorly dog in, or an aged dog or a puppy, we kept it in there for a bit of peace. It was bad in those days in some places in the Highlands with high levels of strays and high rates of parvovirus and distemper.

As more people heard about what we did, more people liked what we were doing. They could see it was really about the animals and purely for the animals and not about us. We were getting support from Dad who paid for the heating oil and income from the rents on a couple of properties. I have never taken a wage at any time. People started being very supportive and donations began coming in.

Then a turning point came when we rescued a dog called Freeway. The newspaper picked up her story and that really put us on the map: it was the best press we could ever have received. They referred to her as 'Greyfriars Bobby of the Highlands'. Freeway was a feral dog living initially under an old biscuit factory warehouse and, when that closed, she moved into a disused underground bunker with her sister, near the slaughter house in Inverness. Various people gave her things to eat, although some people had objected to feeding a feral dog. I and various friends went back and forth providing food for these dogs. Then one day, Freeway's sister got killed on the A9, leaving her on her own and carrying various injuries, probably from vehicles as well.

Both the SSPCA and the Dog Warden tried to capture her but without success. A friend made us a special trap box into which we put every food you could think of, but Freeway would walk round

4

and round the box, wanting the food, but she just was not going in that box. I had a really good friend called Muriel and she and her husband Sandy had taken Freeway's mother from us when she was in a truly dreadful condition, covered in ticks and with a burnt nose. Muriel spent hours on the Longman estate trying to capture Freeway and, because the box was quite difficult to manage on your own, she got herself shut in it. She managed to get out before I arrived but maintained that Freeway was standing watching, in amazement, thinking "what a dork"! No matter what we baited it with, Freeway would not go in.

Over three or four years, we rescued around thirty of Freeway's puppies but we just could not catch her. When the puppies were too young to come out of the hole, Muriel and I would hang down into the hole offering food for the puppies. For about a week to ten days in the run-up to taking the puppies for good, we would go in the morning, pick up the puppies and bring them home where we could worm them, feed them and check their health. We would leave food for Freeway so that she had an easy day without having to go back and forth finding food for herself and the pups. In the evening, we would take them back to the hole where Freeway would look after them for the night. She watched everything we did, never showing any sign of aggression, as if she understood we were helping. When the pups were old enough we took them, much to her relief, since by seven weeks old they were wandering around Harbour Road.

Eventually, Freeway was caught because I saw her and a Golden Retriever mating on the side of the railway line and we swooped! Dave, who was with me, put a canvas bag over Freeway and hoisted her over his shoulder, where she promptly did her business. The Golden Retriever shot off like a rocket in case he was the next one for the canvas bag. A council worker told us that on one occasion, he had seen ten dogs trailing along after Freeway when she was in season.

That first day, 4th July 1986, when we caught Freeway, we put her in a crate at our home but had no way of knowing what to expect. I cooked chicken for her and put it in the crate. I sat watching her and she sat staring at the food but not touching it. When I went out of the room and came back, it was all gone. Whilst Muriel had kept one of Freeway's puppies and called it Muffin, I had kept two called Scruffy and Lassie, and so I took her into the house and let her and her offspring meet in the spare bedroom. The first time I went to give her a kiss on the nose it was too early in our relationship and she snapped at me. I wagged my finger at her and told her very sternly, "You never do that again, never!" and walked out, shutting the door behind me. She never did it again and she absolutely loved kisses and a fuss. The vet confirmed that she was not fit to have more puppies so she was dressed.

Freeway was very much my dog and I was her world, although she was fond of my mother when there was food around. My dad bought a brand new Land Rover and one day, when Freeway was left sitting in the back, I stopped to chat to folk heading into the kennels and then came out cuddling a wee Jack Russell puppy that needed to be taken to the vet. When I opened the car door Freeway had ripped the cover of the front seat to shreds: the green-eyed monster had struck and she had a definite way of making her displeasure clear! On a previous occasion when left, she had taken the stuffing out of an armchair and was found sitting in the midst of it all, stuffing on her nose, in her ears and everywhere else. On the anniversary of her third year at Woodend, she, Scruffy and Muffin had a celebration party, cake and all. Sadly, Lassie was no longer with us but Scruffy lived to be ten years and Muffin to be thirteen. Freeway died in 1991, age unknown but the last four years of her life had been wonderful. She and her puppies were laid to rest at Woodend where the good life had begun for them. Muriel says, "Not a day goes by but our thoughts turn to them and not even time can diminish the loss of such wonderful companions." It is comforting to know that descendants of Freeway must be living with families all over the north.

I remember one day, the whole family were through in the kitchen having a cup of tea when the phone rang and it was the council in Dingwall. They told me that they were going to put out a contract to have strays taken into care, but if we wanted to apply for this we would need to build a proper kennel not the sheds we were using. They gave us no financial help to build the kennels but we managed to have it built and looking wonderful within three or four months with the help of my dad and other family members

*Freeway enjoying her party with her son, Mr Scruffy, and daughter,
Muffin the 2nd and me.*

who he took off other building work in order to complete it. When it was finished, in October 1986, I remember looking at it and wondering why they built so many pens because they would never be full. We were thrilled when we were awarded the contract and the kennel has always been full from the moment it opened. It looked so good that people asked if we would board dogs but that was not what we were about.

Initially, we didn't need any permission for what we were doing but once we had built the kennels then we had to comply with regulations and we had inspections from SSPCA, a fire officer and, from memory, I think it involved a vet too. Nobody ever objected to what we were doing, not as far as I am aware. We never had complaints about the barking but then if a dog is barking at night there is a reason, so one of us would get up and go see.

Sometimes I have a wee regret about leaving paid employment in an office because I could get holidays and, if necessary, I could be off sick. All that stopped when it was just Mum and me doing nearly everything here. I liked the job in Inverness and the people I worked with: they became friends and I was earning good money, but life is not all about you. If you can do something for those who need help, then just go for it! I can't imagine any other life. I am used to being surrounded by loads of animals.

The council asked us questions like "what would we do if a dog was really uncontrollably aggressive or very ill", as if they thought we would never put a dog down. We knew there would be occasions when we had to do that and it is a fact of life when you are running a kennel. Sometimes, the Dog Warden would bring in six dogs in a day and five of them would be reclaimed by their owners but then the next day another six would be brought in. A number of these were not healthy animals and we had to be always on the look-out for infectious diseases. Fortunately, nowadays with the advent of vaccinations we do not see the levels of parvovirus and distemper which were dreadful diseases.

I remember clearly, an old gentleman who had a heart of gold but was not able to care properly for the animals he took in. We took from him a litter of ten puppies with the worst mange I have ever seen. They didn't have a hair on their bodies and were covered in wet mange, plus their bellies were totally distended with

Sandy with Freeway's mother, Muffin the 1st.

worms. When I collected them at 10pm, there were ten little pairs of eyes pleading up at me. We made them as comfortable as we could overnight and fed them. I knew they were in a very bad way and I had them up to the vet the next morning even before the clinic had opened. The vet took one look at what was in the car boot and said that we could not keep these puppies, because of their awful condition, and they needed to be put to sleep. This was not the ending we wanted and is something I cannot forget.

Running the kennel was a huge learning curve. A lot of people donated food to the cats and dogs, which was a tremendous help but there were always vet's bills. Eventually, Mum's and Dad's reserves of money were all used up. But money was needed for other essentials. We realised, for example, that we needed insurance in case a dog got out and caused an accident or bit someone. We have never actually had a dog get out and cause an accident but we did have one get out and chase sheep, fortunately our own, and it was all my sister and I could do to get it back under control. We have had someone bitten but they had been advised against what they were doing but chose to ignore the advice.

Of course, we must not forget the cats. The cats are kept in the huge barn that my mum used to keep the hens in. The barn is divided up so that the feral are separated from the non-feral, but they live in communal groups and seem to get along fine that way. I find that amazing because in my own house we have three cats that live on our bed all day and three that live in the kitchen, but if any of the bedroom cats go to the kitchen and visa versa there is plenty spitting. At the moment, we have a wee kitten being cared for in the kitchen and the kitchen cats are not amused by this 'thing' in their territory.

We did once get some financial support for dealing with a colony of feral cats up on the North West coast, but it took us some time to capture the lot and get them neutered. Feral cats in the wild can lead dreadful lives. For example, when their teeth are bad and they cannot eat they die a slow death and when they cannot hunt, through age or disability, they starve. If there is a cat fight when they are out in the wild and they get wounds that become infected there is no human to treat them so, again, it is a horrible death. At this moment in time, we keep forty or so feral cats and even after neutering we do not release them back into the wild. They live as a well fed, warm and cared for community.

Things have changed in so many ways and mainly for the better. Now that cats should be microchipped it means we can return them back with their owners quickly, so long as they have kept their details up to date, and that has been a really good thing. But there are still plenty of feral cats and we believe that there is an increase in feral dogs. We know of three at present, getting regular reports of sightings but we have never been able to catch any of them.

Chapter 2

A Typical Day at MAA

My typical day does not exist since no two days are ever the same. Usually, Graham and I start about 7am dealing with our own animals, the many cats in the cattery and the large animals and birds outside. Any medicines are given and one or other of us will often have to go off to the vet, twice sometimes in one day and, if we have a sudden admission of a stray that needs attention, we are off to the vet again.

Things are cropping up all the time and it can be absolute chaos, so you can never plan the day. For example, when the paperwork starts to mount up I think I will get a quiet period the next day but, by the end of that day, not one piece of paper has been touched. I need to spend a lot of time researching potential sources of money through grants, writing applications and sending thank-you letters. We are back and forward to the bank or the accountant and to our food suppliers. Every day, decisions have to be made quickly, unexpected visitors dealt with and repairs carried out before they get any worse. I do talks to groups such as cubs or SWI and I now enjoy doing this, although in the beginning I was so nervous I could hardly speak. I would guess that 95% of the people in those groups are really interested in what goes on here and want greater insight into how we operate.

The telephone is constantly ringing. People seem to think that we have a receptionist whose job is just to deal with all these phone calls, and there are many, many calls each day. We could not afford to have another member of staff, so I have no choice but to field all the calls. I got a telephone call this week from a woman who was irate that she had left a message and not received a call back. I apologised and explained that it was nothing personal since I probably had not got around to a number of calls for various reasons. She eventually stopped shouting and made an arrangement to come in and have a look around with a view to rehoming a dog.

Once the centre is closed to the public at 3pm, and staff have gone off duty, Graham and I try to spend a bit of time with our own animals and to make a meal. But that does not always go to plan. For example, yesterday we had just started our meal when someone arrived to collect their dog, the dog warden having brought it in the day before, and this involves paperwork. We sat down again and the police arrived with a dog that had been involved in a seizure, asking if we could take him. This involves quite a lengthy process and a lot of paperwork as well as getting the worried animal settled into the kennel block, fed and watered.

In the late afternoon, Graham and I, with my friend Margaret helping, start giving the centre animals their second meal of the day and, in the kennel block, letting them out to spend a penny and sometimes have a second walk. Sometimes, a dog has had a wee 'accident' in their pen, so we clean them up before bedtime and settle them into a nice warm bed for the night, checking that they have plenty of water. If we get a chance, we sit down for a while before bed at around 10.30pm but you cannot guarantee that. And it is not unusual to have the police arrive during the night with an animal or to get a phone call that needs us to go out. Mind you, we might already be up if we are doing two hourly feeding very young animals.

I honestly do not know how we would cope here without Graham. There is something that needs doing every day and he is on call day and night. When the drains have been unblocked, then it is the gutter's turn to overflow or the tumble dryer to misbehave - just one thing after another that he needs to attend to, as well as all his work with the animals. It would take me all day to list everything he does around MAA. If, on a rare occasion, we go out for a meal in the evening, maybe celebrating a family event, there has to be someone here who can act if there is an emergency. My friend Margaret who lives nearby always helps out or a couple of family members do this for us. Of course, I always have the phone with me!

Not infrequently, we have to deal with dissatisfied members of the public during the day. People get angry because their dog has been brought in by the police or dog warden. They get angry that they are expected to pay the uplift fee of £25, which goes direct to the council not the kennel, and angry that they had to come all this way to get their own dog back. If I can get that £25 uplift fee for the council I do, but if the situation is really unpleasant then I am not going to get into trouble for the sake of it. I got bitten by a furious woman once and when my cousin heard the commotion he raced up the field to help and he also sustained an injury. And it was quite a bite! We held on to her until the police came and she was charged but I was really shaken up. Clearly, she was stressed about her dog having been taken into the kennel but for a human to bite another human being is a bit extreme. However, some years later she met me in a car park and apologised for her behaviour, which meant such a lot to me.

It is not necessarily that the person coming to reclaim their dog just does not have the money. A local farmer, who is certainly not without funds, went mad when asked for the uplift fee. The dog had been straying for a couple of days and could have caused a serious accident if the warden had not caught it, but that was irrelevant to him and he just wanted his dog back free of charge. People do not seem to appreciate that the uplift fee goes to the council and, unless they make a donation, MAA gets nothing for looking after their dog.

Sometimes our day goes from bad to worse with one phone call. We were involved in a case where a man telephoned to say that his dogs had started fighting and one of them had been badly hurt. He claimed he had no transport and no means of getting the animal to a vet. The SSPCA inspector was out of the area on that day, so Graham and I drove many miles that evening to collect the animal, having first told the vet at Conon that I would be bringing in an injured animal but it would be after they had closed for the evening. The dog was covered in puncture wounds and in a very bad way. When we had got it into the car, I asked where the other dog that had caused these wounds was and he showed me. He had

13

used a machete to split up the fight and in doing so had inflicted a horrific injury on the second dog. He had not been going to bring the second dog out to us to take for veterinary help.

We got both dogs to the vet having rung ahead to tell them just how bad the situation was and the kind of injuries we were bringing in. The SSPCA took over the case and the second dog was put to sleep because of its condition. This became a court case and we attended the court. The owner got community service, which was completely inadequate, and I was raging in the court, Graham trying all the time to quieten me down. Since the man did not complete his community service he went to gaol, unfortunately only for a few weeks. Although he was banned from owning another dog there were still two dogs in that house but they were, apparently, his wife's!

One Sunday evening, it was a dark night, and somebody had abandoned a cockerel which was, according to the lady who telephoned, going to get eaten by a fox. Since it was dark, my cousin came down from Tore to go with me and we captured the cockerel.

I had done all the feeding before I left and the kennels were locked up. However, when my cousin had left I saw the kennel doors were open and I knew Mum would not have had any cause to go into the kennels while I was off catching the cockerel. When I looked, someone had kicked the door in and stolen two dogs. The police came out and took details and I telephoned my cousin to come back and make the door safe again. This was all before we had internet, so I telephoned everyone I could think of to ask them to be on the lookout for these two dogs. I went on Moray Firth Radio and talked to the local papers. Three days later, I got a call to say that the two dogs had been dumped on an estate in Inverness. I think the amount of publicity had made the thieves realise they were never going to be able to be seen with these dogs and nor was anyone else.

Having dogs stolen is a terrible thing to happen and those were amongst the worst three days of my life. If they had been honest, they would have gone through the usual process required prior to rehoming an animal. I could guess, but did not know what they planned to do with these dogs because they had not just taken any

The cockerel who lived to crow another day.

dog: they had chosen two Staffordshire Bull Terriers! The kennel block now has additional security doors made of metal so that nobody can break in.

The only other time we had a dog stolen was when a young lad took his own puppy back. His puppy had been brought in by the dog warden the previous day. He ran with the puppy in his arms and I gave chase but could not catch up with him. He could just have gone through the usual process to reclaim and I would have had to give him his dog back since it was within the seven-day period. However, he acted on the spur of the moment. We knew where he lived and contacted him. He apologised for his behaviour and, as far as we know, has taken better care of his dog since then.

One of our dog walkers, Colin, was walking this very quiet calm dog that had come in from Fort Augustus. Colin tripped, dropping the lead and the dog shot off. That was about 10.30am and we were all out searching for this dog. My brother-in-law came home for lunch at 12.30pm to say that there was a dog going across the

Kessock Bridge trailing a lead behind it. I telephoned a couple of friends in Inverness explaining the situation. One of them was a bus driver who also drove a taxi, so he spread the word around his taxi colleagues. One of them spotted the dog heading out the Drum Road and it became clear that the dog was heading home to Fort Augustus. On the evening of the second day, I was out searching and John, another dog walking friend was in his car going up and down the same road. Eventually, I spotted the dog and managed to turn him up the Abriachan road where we parked the cars and just sat there talking quietly to the dog. He was so exhausted, thirsty and hungry that he was glad to be caught and got willingly into John's cars.

Back in 2001 I had a very untypical day. I had taken a day off to go up Ben Nevis with my cousin, a novelty in itself but when I got back and opened the mail, mainly bills, I discovered one that said 'Prime Minister's Office' on the envelope. It asked if I would be willing to accept the honour of an MBE but I was not to tell anyone. Of course I would accept it and, of course, I told my mother but she thought it was someone playing a joke on me. Once she accepted that this was genuine, she was so excited since she loved anything 'royal' and we would have to go to London to receive it.

When we got to the airport at Dalcross, my sister, myself and two nieces got through the security point but mother, who had never been on a plane before, could not find her ticket. She was adamant that she would stay back whilst we all went down to London but, eventually, after much searching, she found the ticket tucked inside her furry boot and got through. We all had an amazing time when I received the MBE from HRH Prince Charles. It was a bit embarrassing because it was at the time when issues with the genetically modified crops were in the news. He asked me if the protests around the Black Isle had affected me and I shyly replied 'no'. However, just a few weeks later, I was caught in the GM field near Munlochy, nailed to the floor by a German Shepherd dog and put in a cell for the weekend. Thank goodness this was not before the meeting with Prince Charles!

To finish off the special day, we went to see Starlight Express. This was not to my mother's taste. My mother refused to go down the steps to sit in the seats we were allocated and announced to the usher that she was going to sit where she was. He kindly told her to sit wherever she wanted but when she sat she complained loudly that the seats were not very comfortable. The usher replied "You haven't folded the seat down yet, madam."

We had hardly had anything to eat in London and coming back on the plane we were offered a meal and drinks. In those days there was no catering for a vegetarian, so I just picked what I could off the plate and left the rest. When they came around offering drinks Mum said she did not want any alcohol. I persuaded her to take anything they offered, considering the price we were charged for the flight. She took a vodka and they were not mean when pouring it. She got so drunk on it that you would have thought she had been drinking throughout the whole flight. At one point, I turned the air above our seats on and Mum asked if someone had opened a window: this was at several thousand feet up, but she was new to flying!

Sadly, Mum died a couple of months before Alexis and I went to a Royal Garden Party at Holyrood Palace. We were so proud to be there - two girl crofters from the Black Isle. Mum would have been in her element seeing the Royals and eating tiny little sandwiches and tarts!

There is just no typical day, so much goes on and so much goes on behind the scenes that few people know about. We cannot afford more staff and we are constantly looking at the bank account. My worst fear, apart from the money running out, is that both Graham and I would be involved in a fatal accident. What happens to our own animals, especially the three dogs that are so old and worn out that they would just have to be put down if we could not look after them? They say nobody is indispensable, but I worry that MAA might not continue and it must.

Chapter 3

An Expensive Business

Averaged out, it costs between £2,000 and £3,000 each week to run Munlochy Animal Aid. Most people gasp when they hear this but they do not realise that on any given day there are around 150 creatures being cared for, huge food and heating bills, veterinary bills and professional services fees such as farrier and accountant.

In the early days it was a tremendous financial struggle. Trying to decide should we pay the vet's bill, oil bill, or food bill and sometimes we did not have enough money to pay everything that was due. The vets at Conon were amazing at that time and it would not be the first time that a cheque had bounced. We always paid eventually, but it was quite a struggle. My mother and I would sometimes spend the evening trying to work out how we could get a bit more money and then the next day a cheque for £50 would arrive in the post and we were saved. It was just Mum and I and Dad digging deep into his pocket but it was really hard. Sometimes, dad would say we just could not keep on doing this, but he always found some more cash to help us out.

We have had really bad times when we were down to the last bag of food but no animal has ever gone to bed hungry and was never cold. When more people knew about us, especially after the press gave a lot of publicity to our rescue of the dog we called Freeway, more people became generous to us. We have tried a lot of ways of getting food cheaply. For instance, at one time we could get tripe for free but we had to hang it up and cut slices off. Obviously, the dogs liked it but I, being a vegetarian, found it absolutely disgusting and try as I may, I just could not keep working with it. We used to get out-of-date meat pies given to us which the dogs also enjoyed.

Once, we approached the fishing boats in Ullapool and ask if they could sell us any fish, but cheaply. One fisherman asked what we would collect the fish in and we said we had a trailer. He filled our trailer with mackerel for free, so long as we got there for 4am. We had to get this fish home to freeze and we cooked it in a Burco boiler. The cats enjoyed it but nowadays, there are so many restrictions on what can and cannot be given away, and all the hoops that companies have to go through, that it becomes too much of a problem to go scavenging around for food supplies.

We buy a lot of foodstuff from an animal feed supplier in Inverness and try to make our journey a monthly one. We discipline ourselves to have a list of what we need and to stick to it. It is all too easy to go in wanting three things and see a couple of other things that would be nice to bring back, but you just cannot do that when you are buying for a charity like this. You must need the stuff you are buying and nothing else and use the stuff you have bought, with no waste. We buy our cat food from Tesco, costing around £600 a month, which is about the cheapest around and they deliver it direct to us. We get clubcard points and discounts so, at the moment, this is our best option.

Any major expenses can be budgeted for such as kennel alterations but, of course, there are unexpected expenses. For example, one week the industrial washing machine broke down costing £3,500 and then, a few weeks later, the kennel heating system broke down costing £4,500. The new ones will probably last longer than I will, so, fingers crossed, I will not need to replace these again. In the same financial year, we had to build new outdoor runs since the old ones were rusty and no longer safe. Money just keeps going out!

There are the necessary expenses such as regular checks on our electricity connections since, although the kennel is built in such a way that it would not easily catch fire, we take no chances, especially after the horrendous events that followed the fire at Battersea Dogs Home. We have to have an evacuation plan just in case and there is always someone with keys on site day and night for any emergency. If there is barking at night one or other of us will be up to check what is wrong.

As the charity grew, so did the complexity of paperwork and it was a steep learning curve for me. For instance, I had never employed staff until ten years ago and was new to all that this involves. I had to get it right for all our sakes. The first member of staff we had was a girl who arrived one day on the off chance. She said she was looking for a job and it had to be with animals. Now we have two full-time and two part-time staff who work predominantly in the kennels. Employment became more and more technical and complicated and I mistakenly sent in a set of figures twice causing one member of staff to get a letter telling her she owed £2,000 in unpaid taxes! So, after that I handed the staff side employment issues over to an accountant. The accountant helps with tax, the Charity Commissioner, and all financial record keeping which has to be 100% right so that it can be open to inspection at any time. We also engage a solicitor if necessary but I cannot remember South Forrest Solicitor's billing us for anything to do with MAA.

Our annual veterinary bill can be enormous. With that number of animals there is usually one or other in need of treatment and sometimes we can be back and forth to the vet two or three times a day. There is no 'cut-off point' in relation to what operations or treatments I would have done to one of our residents. We have to take into consideration factors such as likely outcome; what the animal's quality of life will be afterwards; and issues around the animal itself.

The animal itself is the most important consideration and what is best for it. It is difficult to rehome an animal if it has ongoing health problems requiring expensive diets, daily medications and various other costly needs. We recently had a lovely German Shepherd handed over to the kennels but despite putting him on a very expensive diet, he was not improving and looked really tired. For a young dog he should have had a spark in him but he just did not: it was as if a light had gone out and his life was not enjoyable. One of our own dogs has the same health problem but we have been able to get it under control, although it will shorten her life. She is going on for ten years and the vets did not think that she would make it to seven months, so it can be done but we just knew it was not in that dog's best interest to put him through all that and not get a good result. He would probably have had to remain in the kennel for a very long time. Difficult decisions have to be made when you run a rescue centre.

If an animal needs major surgery, with all the follow-up, then they are better off in a home environment than here. We can care for them afterwards in our isolation block where it is quieter but it is not a home environment. Sometimes, friends and volunteers will foster the animal until it is recovered but, as they will tell you, sometimes these animals spend the rest of their life with them. One couple have had a series of dogs that they have cared for as a 'temporary' measure and, as yet, they have never brought any of them back. Five years later they could still be heard telling people that the dog they were walking was only staying with them for two weeks!

We have operated a free micro-chipping scheme for a number of years and this has made a big difference to our ability to reunite strays with their owners. What most people do not know is that we pay some veterinary fees, especially neutering, for people from all across Highland who are on a really low income, adore their pet but have an emergency veterinary need arise. We do not pay the whole bill unless there are very special reasons for it. We often have people begging for financial help to have an elderly or sick pet put to sleep because they cannot afford to pay for this essential final treatment. In a perfect world people would not have an animal if they could not afford its veterinary bills but we do not live in a perfect world and people's circumstances can change overnight: they lose their job, family and home but do not want to lose their pet.

If I were to be made homeless, I would not be parted from my dogs and many people are like that. I remember an old gentleman in Inverness living in a wee caravan which was classed as illegally parked. He lived with three dogs that were so very important to him. Whilst this gentleman was shopping, the council moved in and took the caravan away, leaving the three dogs sitting on a duvet where the caravan had been. He would not go into the accommodation available to him because the dogs could not go too.

We heard about what had happened because someone from the press contacted us and we went over to find him absolutely distraught. We offered to take the dogs so that he could go into the accommodation until he got sorted out and could have his beloved dogs back. He refused and someone gave him a wee tent which he and the dogs moved in to. It was near an industrial estate and some of the night-watchmen would bring him in to their site to make him hot drinks and we were going over with food.

Then my father came up with a plan which involved getting the gentleman to tell the council, late on a Friday afternoon, that he needed access to his caravan since he had got someone to move it and somewhere to put it. So, my father hitched up the caravan and towed it about 500 yards down the road to a bit of land where he could be tucked in, no trouble to anyone and that was him all set up again with his dogs. Eventually, the council just accepted that this was a solution, albeit not of their choosing and, since they would not let him onto the traveller's site run by the council because he was not classed as a bona fide traveller, it was the only solution.

However, we got up a petition and so many people signed it that the council allowed him to move onto the traveller's site. We had always been involved with the travellers, going back and forth to the site and so we were able to keep an eye on him and his dogs. We help people as well as animals but it is an expensive business and we deal with vets all across Highlands when helping people on low incomes to get treatment for their pets.

Over the last forty years we have had all kinds of creatures. We mostly come into contact with cats and dogs, both the pet and feral kinds, but we have had a number of wild animals such as wildcats, goats, otters, seals, hedgehogs, rabbits, ferrets, frogs, squirrels and birds of every kind. We have had sheep, horses and pigs and some rather exotic guests. This all means that we have to have different foodstuff, the right accommodation and access to expert knowledge. We are a registered croft, although we do not get any grants, so we can take all sorts so long as we maintain standards and keep appropriate records of the numbers of animals and so on.

Chapter 4

Making Ends Meet

We get our income from various sources. For example, the annual fete on the last Saturday in August always generates a welcome income and, this year was exceptional in that we raised £11,500 just from generosity. This was down to it being the 40th anniversary for MAA; the weather was lovely; there was a fantastic crowd spending everything they could afford; and lots of our volunteers pulling out all the stops to run stalls, sell raffle tickets, and enter dogs in the competitions. There is tremendous generosity shown by local businesses and individuals who donate raffle prizes and, this year, we held our first auction on the day. The fete requires a great deal of planning and organisation but, fortunately, most of our volunteers have done it year after year so they know what they are doing and it runs smoothly.

At the fun day we have baking, bric-a-brac, music including our piper and keyboard player, and a barbecue which sold over 300 burgers this year. Graham's mother and father, Moira and Neil, help no end and Moira does an astonishing amount of baking which she sells at the Moray Firth car boot sales as well as the fun day. People actually come along to those events to seek out Moira's baking which raises so much money.

Lots of people bring dogs to the fun day including those who have been resident at some point. Some people just come along because they have heard it is a lot of fun. There is plenty of parking in a nearby field and a local garage owner provides a shuttle bus which allows both dogs and human on board.

The dog show is far from a serious show. We do have best pedigree and best puppy but we also have lots of silly classes like the dog most like its owner, the waggiest tail or the cutest eyes. A retired vet does all the judging and this year we had 297 entries. Nobody really cares who wins, they are just all having fun, both dogs and owners. There is a class called best rescue dog and that is for animals that have had a pretty rough time and been through a lot. The dog will now be doing well in a new home and I judge that class because I know what that particular dog was like when it first came to us.

At Christmas we tend to get more donations of food and treats for the animals but I do not think people really realise just how much this means to us, nor how incredibly important it was in the early days. We are given bedding, towels, collars and leads, food bowls and all manner of goods that can be put to good use here or sold to raise money.

We now have 'Friends of Munlochy Animal Aid' who are people who make regular donations. This regular source of monthly income means we can budget and plan ahead. Although most of the Friends are likely to be popping into the centre every once in a while, they are kept up-to-date with the work of MAA through an annual update newsletter. I do not do thank you letters to these regular givers because they say they would prefer I spent the money on the animals and not on stamps and envelopes. Some charities give all sorts of free gifts like pens and stickers, but our Friends would probably ask how much it cost to produce all that and would not the money be put to better use on food for the animals?

We received £5,000 from the Tesco store in Dingwall who allowed us to be one of the three charities that shoppers could vote for by dropping tokens into a box. We had the most tokens, so we got the money. In fact, they said we had one of the highest numbers of tokens they had seen. Local people do support local charities. We have car boot sales and a permanent bookstall in the Inverness Co-op store that very kindly let us have a bit of space near the checkouts where the books sit alongside an honesty box for a donation. This is a valuable source of income and is managed by two of our volunteers who keep it topped up with books donated to MAA. Sometimes, people will raise money through sponsor-

The Dog Show at the MAA fete.

ship and Cathy, one of our vets, completed a sponsored cycle ride from Lands End to John O'Groats, all with no back-up support, just her tent and her bike.

We have a team of volunteers who will collect money when a store or precinct kindly allows us to have a collecting point. My friend, Margaret, spends hours contacting potential collection points and then organising the rota of volunteers. People will actually come up to the stand and empty their purses of change. Sometimes we get a cheque written out and very often the volunteers hear stories about animals that the person has taken from MAA and the difference it has made to their lives. How much money is generated from a collection is variable but, recently, we raised nearly £800 during a three-day collection in Morrisons supermarket in Inverness.

We have food collection boxes in various stores and some of our volunteers empty them regularly. We use a lot of this food for the animals here but times are hard and more and more folk are using food banks, so we donate some cat or dog food to these. It must be an awful worry to be struggling to feed yourself and your bairns but also to feed your pet.

I once raised money by getting sponsorship to take a flying lesson at Dalcross. Lots of people sponsored me because I think they thought they would never have to pay up because I would chicken out. What they probably did not know was that I had been in a plane before and loved it. Dad had bid in a charity auction with Moray Firth Radio for a helicopter ride for me and my sister, and he was successful, so I knew I loved flying and would not chicken out. If I had the money, I would fly again.

We regularly receive collections raised at funerals when it had been the deceased wish, or that of their family, to support the charity. Maybe they had taken an animal from us at some point or maybe they just knew about us and the work we do. Sometimes we get legacies when people die and that constitutes a tremendous, unexpected windfall for us. Quite often it is people we have never come into direct contact with who leave us money in their will. Our first legacy came from a man we did know and that money made so much difference to us because, at that time, I was really struggling to keep the place going at the same time as coping with unwell elderly parents. The money meant survival at that time and the only condition he had put on the legacy was that we had to be a registered charity so that we did not have to pay tax on his money!

At one time, I did not have the confidence to approach anyone to ask for money. I did not know how you went about asking for money and did not even have a computer. I am working on fundraising all the time now, doing research into companies and organisations that will give various amounts of money. I send out lots of begging letters and grant applications. Even when I have posted a grant application there is no guarantee that it will even get accepted for consideration. Animal charities do not do so well when it comes to getting grants from big businesses and it may only be as little as one in forty applications that are successful.

We were recently invited to an event where local charities were able to talk to businessmen and women from a dozen big companies. Of all the people there that day, not one would give to an animal charity. Some people have the impression that all we are doing is playing a game with cuddly dogs and cats. They do not realise that the police will bring in a dog at 2am when its owner has been arrested. There is nowhere else for the police to take that dog. It could be with us for weeks or even months, depending on what happens to the owner. In the last couple of weeks we have taken a dog in this situation and it is in lovely condition and is a clearly a much loved pet. Where else would the police take it if MAA was not here? If the owner goes to prison and has very little to look forward to but the hope he can have his dog back when he is released, we have no way of recouping the money it costs to care for the animal.

This week we had a call to say that someone had collapsed and been rushed to hospital and nobody was able to take their dog, so we made a space for it since it had to be taken within the next thirty minutes. The elderly owner has to know that his dog is being cared for in a warm, safe environment because it is his only companion. It will be here for him to come home to or we will find it a loving home should he decide he is no longer able to offer it that care. Either way, he will have peace of mind.

We are an animal charity but we work with the community, supporting people in different circumstances, so we are helping humans but because we are classed as an animal charity we just do not do as well when it comes to grants. Some of the grants require the general public to vote for the charity and we are in competition with charities down south with many more potential voters. I have to spend a lot of time getting as many people as possible up here in the Highlands and Islands to go on line and vote for us since this is increasingly the way funding decisions are made.

If we have a dog brought in by the council we cannot rehome it for seven days, which allows time for the owner to reclaim their pet. Once the dog has been in for more than seven days MAA can bill the council for that week's kennelling fees, which is £12 per night. After seven days that dog becomes our responsibility and we may have vet bills, including neutering fees and microchipping costs, but the council does not pay any contribution or retainer fees. If we have a dog in for just a night or two, we have no way of getting any money for its care, including food, and if that dog came in with an injury there are likely veterinary fees. Some owners make donations to the kennel if they retrieve their dog but if nobody comes to reclaim it MAA gets no financial help. We have been running the stray dog kennelling service for Highland Council for 25 years now. We are grateful to have a source of income but we are starting to think that the arrangement might benefit from a review.

Chapter 5

The Dogs and Cats

By far the most numerous animals to come into Munlochy Animal Aid are dogs and cats. Between June 2017 and June 2018 we took in 357 dogs and 72 cats. It is very rare for the kennels not to be full and quite often it is so full that some are put in a kennel with another dog that they get along with. Some of the smaller ones have to go into crates on a short-term basis until a kennel is available.

The reasons why owners pass their animals over to us are varied. Their circumstances change or relationships break up and neither partner can keep the pet, or maybe money becomes an issue when unemployment strikes and the owner cannot afford to keep their pet anymore. We often encounter owners who have developed health problems, frailty or disability and they have had to make a heart-breaking decision to hand over their pet. Everyone is sad when someone, through age or infirmity, has no choice but to hand over a beloved animal especially if they have had it for a long time.

There are, however, people who treat animals like a disposable commodity. They might bring in a dog they have had for years saying they do not want it anymore because they are going on holiday or because they are moving to a new house with nice new carpets. It is their choice and there might be things they are not telling me, but I am not here to judge and I will always take the animal, no matter what the story.

When someone wants to hand an animal in, we make it as easy as possible. We might say they have to wait a few days or a week, just until we have the space, whether it is a cat, rabbit, dog or whatever. We always tell them that we guarantee we will take the animal. We like to get as much information as we can. We want to know the history. We want to know whether the animal is people-friendly, animal-friendly, has any health issues and whether they have been neutered, inoculated and microchipped. These are all the kind of questions that the potential new owner is going to want answers to. Sometimes we get the whole story but sometimes it is not so close to the truth for whatever reason: they are telling us what they want to tell us in order to solve their problem. For example, sometimes people tell us things that are quite damning for the dog such as saying the dog has bitten a child but when we ask for more details they modify the statement by saying it was not the dog's fault because of what the child was doing to it. You have to try to read between the lines.

Sometimes it makes me angry when I hear why someone is passing an animal over to us but I would never lose my cool until I have got the animal. The priority is getting the animal into a safe place, so I control my feelings. My mother one day lost a dog because of what she did and it has stayed in my mind forever. Someone came in asking if we would take a dog. The woman was parked across the road and when we went out to see the dog we could not believe what we were seeing. The condition of the dog was so bad it was unbelievable. My mother just lost the plot straight away and the woman drove off with the dog, so it had lost its chance of help. But, fortunately, I did know who they were and so the SSPCA were involved and the dog was put down because it was so bad there was nothing else they could do. My mother learned something that day and I learned to think before I react. It was utter shock at seeing the state of the poor creature that made her react as she did.

Any person who takes on an animal is accepting responsibility for that animal. What makes me really angry is people who are totally irresponsible. For instance, someone brought a cat in that was so heavily pregnant that it gave birth two days later. The cat had never been microchipped, never been to a vet, never had flea treatment nor inoculations and it was handed over with no emotion. It was just, 'Take this!' It was just a nuisance and a problem that was being got rid of. But, to give the woman credit, it was far

How do I get out of here?

better to bring the animal in to us than just abandon it to starve or freeze and, at the end of the day, I am not here to sit in judgement: my role is to get the animal away to where it can receive the care it needs. Once an animal has been signed over to us, I do sometimes try to explain the kind of commitment you need to have if you own an animal and maybe that person will think about this in future, but maybe not.

If an animal comes here in a very bad condition, the first thing I do is take it to the vet and notify the SSPCA. By law, I am not allowed to refuse to give an animal back to its owner within that first seven-day period unless a vet states that the condition merits it remaining here and not being returned to the owner. The SSPCA will follow up such cases but the animal will remain with us at MAA.

One night, when the temperature had dropped to around -15C, we found a lead tied to our wheelie bin. Clearly, there had been a dog on the end of it but it was not until the next day that a Staffordshire Bull Terrier was spotted in the wood. It took us three days to catch that dog. We tried all kinds of food in the dog trap and, in the end, Graham went into town and bought a fish supper, the smell of which the dog could not resist. After some time with us he went to a lovely home and did very well but I could not get over the incredible cruelty of leaving a fine-skinned dog on a night like that. Why not just knock on our door and ask us to take it?

We ask people to sign the animal over to us, in other words, they relinquish ownership and included in that is their need to confirm that they are the owner and no other ownership interest or claim exists. We had a very sad situation where a family had split up a couple of years ago and whilst the woman had moved south, the male partner had stayed up here with the dog. Eventually, the man's circumstances changed so that the dog was being left on its own all day and he recognised that this was not good for the animal. He brought his dog into Munlochy and signed it over. Fairly quickly, the dog got a very good home but unfortunately was involved six months later in an accident and died. However, the man's previous partner turned up wanting her dog back, although she had not seen the animal for two years. She was very angry and dealt with this by going to the press claiming we had taken and rehomed *her* dog, a family dog, without her permission.

It is very difficult to prove that the animal the person is handing over is theirs. The good thing nowadays is that with microchipping we can scan the animal. If the records do not tally with the person handing the animal in then we would question them. We recently had a situation where a cat was handed in. It was a gorgeous pedigree cat and I put it on Facebook. I received a phone call from someone in Perthshire to say she thought it was her cat. However, it was not registered to her address because she had not got around to updating the details of house moves, which is so very important. She was able to give us details of the breeder and we were able to confirm that the cat was hers and he went back home.

Who can resist those eyes?

We had a dog that had been straying brought in near Christmas time. When I scanned it, the dog was registered to someone in Birmingham. I telephoned the chipping company and they said that this particular dog was recorded as having been stolen from the owner's garden six months ago. I phoned the owner and said we were a stray dog kennel and had Bruno in our care. There was screaming at the end of the phone with shouts of "They've got Bruno, they've got Bruno!" We had to keep the dog for a wee while until his owner could fly up and after a very happy, emotional reunion, took Bruno back down on the train.

When we first started all those years ago, we were constantly out picking up litters of kittens and puppies. They would be poorly, flea ridden, kittens suffering from flu-like symptoms and the puppies with big distended bellies full of worms. We still get litters of puppies that we have to feed two-hourly, day and night, but, fortunately, not so often now. We do not get a lot of sleep when young puppies have to be kept warm and clean and fed and you need to spend a lot of time with them, getting them used to being handled. It is like being a substitute mother for them because the social skills mum would teach still need to be passed on to them. These puppies tend to be very affectionate and make good pets. We never have a job finding homes for puppies anyway but, fortunately for us, some people prefer to rescue an older dog rather than take a puppy.

We have been running neutering schemes for a while now and what a difference this has made to the numbers of kittens and puppies that come in. People come and ask if we can help. Times are hard, vet bills are high and if you just have not got the money to pay, then the scheme is a lifesaver. It takes a lot of money but I believe it is worth it and sometimes, when the owner has a bit of luck, they give us a donation.

Many years ago we started trapping feral cats mainly where the landfill dump used to be in Inverness. There were dozens of feral cats there and you would see wee kittens dying with flu and looking wretched but nobody was doing anything about it. So Dad made trap boxes and we went back and forth for hours trapping these cats. Word got out that we would take feral cats and we would catch them and so it grew and grew. One evening I had already been back and forth to the dump three times when I made the final journey. All three trap boxes were full and it was a squeeze to get them into the van. As I was driving out of the dump, one of the boxes opened and I had a furious feral cat flying around inside the van. Getting it back in the box was a hair-raising half hour I can tell you. My sister, Alexis, and her husband, Mackie, have been very involved with the cats, doing the feeding and cleaning from even before their girls were school age. Alexis has this lovely calm, quiet, gentle way that is exactly what you need for working with feral cats. Nowadays, Graham is very involved with the feral cats too.

We were once as high as seventy feral cats in residence here but we still have forty to fifty of them. They are all health-checked and blood-tested for AIDS and leukaemia and neutered when they come in. They live in two heated cat houses with big beds which they multi-occupy, snuggling up to each other, which is surprising, and with outdoor runs with climbing frames made by Graham and tree trunks to jump on.

Above: Puss enjoying the sunshine.

Left: A contented feral cat.

When you are feeding that number of cats, you need to know that none of them are missing out on what they should get. That comes with experience and you are watching all the time to see if one is hanging back or takes a mouthful of food and then winces because he has a bad tooth or sore gum. If you are working with animals all the time you can spot things that other people might not see. It is like a human mother with ten children who would still know if one of them was not all right. They have enough food that their dishes are never empty so even the wee quiet one who does not want to come to a dish with others around, he still has the chance to come at a different time to eat.

We do have to be diligent because there are all different ages of cat there and all different problems crop up with them. Age is the biggest killer in our cat houses, not illness, but we do sometimes have to have a cat put to sleep. It is rare that one of them just dies and you go in and find a dead animal. When that happens it is a horrible feeling because you feel you have missed something that you should have spotted, although that may not be the case. We had this happen just once in the kennels. It was such a shock when you go to bed at night and every one of them is fine and then in the morning one of them has died. You feel that you have been negligent and missed something but that was not the case. Sudden, unexpected deaths happen with people and it happens with animals.

Our feral cats do tame down to a degree. I think what helps is the fact that we strictly limit the number of people who go into the cat house and they get to know those people and relax around them. Some eventually come to ask for a fuss but it is in their own time and on their own terms. Some will never come closer than a few feet and are always wary. We are not asking anything of that cat, not forcing our attention on it, nor expecting anything of it.

We have a separate cat house for non-feral cats that get health checked and neutered and microchipped if they have not already been done and then rehomed as quickly as possible. It is reasonably easy to rehome a young healthy cat but older cats take a bit longer. Responsible owners look at whether they can afford a pet and with older animals potential owners see vet bills looming. We also offer a boarding cattery service and have done so for nearly thirty years.

At this moment, Graham is doing the majority of the work with our cats so he knows them well. However, this very morning he had to take a wee female cat in to be neutered only to be told that it was a neutered male he had brought in, so he had to come back and get the right cat!

Someone has found a comfy spot to snooze in.

Chapter 6

Every Animal is Different

I do believe that animals have personalities. Pigs, goats, horses, dogs, cats and even rabbits and guinea pigs all have their little individual characteristics.

With our own dogs, one is a bossy little brat; one is so laid back that he is not bothered what goes on; one is a real plodder; two are typical collies and wired to the moon; and one has had so many little issues that we have had to stay on his case continually. With experience, I can sometimes look at a dog, particularly its eyes, and tell an awful lot. Some dogs can look you straight in the eye, whereas others find it hard to do this and it is more difficult to tell what they are really like.

How they behave is not always down to how they have been treated. I once had a dog from when he was about four weeks old and so I knew what experiences he had but if I picked up a floor brush he was petrified. He had never been hit with a brush, so why did he respond like that? There was something in him and I believe that dogs do have quirks in their nature. For instance, some might nip you in the back of your leg but they have never been taught to do that and it is just something in them. They talk about 'Cocker Rage' and we have seen Cocker Spaniels that go from being so nice and docile to showing outrageous behaviour with very little cause, so I think you do get rogue dogs.

Of course, there have been dogs we just could not rehome because of aggression. We give them a long time, sometimes as long as two years to try to come around. You can work away over time with a dog and I will get a feeling if there is potential to turn

Judy, my bossy little brat!

them around. Sometimes we end up taking it into our own home to live out its life.

When we got six German Shepherds all at once from the same source it was quite overwhelming. They had been allowed to form a pack and this had resulted in serious problems. They were not at all easy to handle, especially one of them. For the first two or three weeks, I was the only person who worked with them. I walked each of them twice a day and it was a nerve-racking thing to do because they were suspicious of everybody. When they were together as a pack they were worse but when you walked them one at a time it took away some of their bravado, although each one eyed you with real suspicion. But I was walking these creatures for six or seven hours in the day. If you work too long and closely with a dog they bond with you and the bond they had developed with their original owner, who had got them into the state they were in, was being transferred to me. Graham became involved and then another one of the volunteers, which took the pressure off me and was better for the dogs because they were getting used to being around different people.

They were a whisker away from a destruction order but it became very clear that there was potential there and we turned them around. They all got rehomed and have been wonderful pets though, sadly, they have all now passed away. I was overjoyed the day of the fete when all six of these dogs were brought back by their new owners and I got to hold their leads all together. They had been apart for some time but they clearly all remembered each other and, despite all the noise and activity going on in the dog show ring, they behaved perfectly. It made all the hard work worthwhile and shows what you can do with a dog if you give it time and effort.

The original owner of the German Shepherds had been banned from having a dog for life as a consequence of the way he had treated his dogs. Sometime later, we were asked to take two adult brother and sister Rottweilers and their five puppies. We discovered that they came from the same man, who had subsequently died but by changing his name he had managed to get these Rottweilers. Together with their five puppies they would have formed another pack just as the six German Shepherd Dogs had done. We were able to rehome all of them.

There was a dog with a muzzle on that was left tied up outside a local vet. The dog was behaving really badly and the SSPCA attended but, at that time, had no kennels up here. I took the dog in and I managed to get the muzzle off, which was far from easy since he was behaving in a really aggressive manner. But I vowed he would never have another muzzle put on his face. I called him Ceullie. I would sit outside that kennel with my face right up close to the bars. I would sing, tell him nursery rhymes and talk the biggest load of rubbish. I did not look at him, except down at his feet.

After three or four weeks of me doing this, Ceullie probably started to think that this woman was insane, so he saw no point to keep threatening me. The next step was to let Ceullie out of his pen into the kennel block with me. I locked the outside doors so nobody could come in unexpectedly and then I unlocked his pen. I went into the kitchen and started doing things at the sink, not looking at him but knowing that he was now standing behind me. I got a dish of food and told him to get back in his bed to eat it. I knew that if he started up, I was in a really difficult spot but he just went back in to eat and from that day there was trust between us. Nobody else could get near him.

After a while, I encouraged my friend Margaret, who helped at

Coullie, Flash, Struan, Sally-Ann and Molly with me in the woods.

the kennel, to speak to him and take biscuits to him until, eventually the dog was fine with Margaret and her partner and with my mother. It upset my father that the dog never really took to him since Dad adored all dogs. We could walk the dog but we knew nobody else should come near him, so we had to be very careful when strangers were around. He would walk anywhere without the need for a lead but whenever he saw someone coming he would want to go back on his lead for his own safety and I wanted him on it for that person's safety. When he was out with Margaret one day, a friend of hers came up to them and bent to pet him. She got a nip, so I realised that he was not going to be a dog we could ever rehome, so I kept him. Eventually, Ceullie would take himself off across the field to visit Margaret and her partner who lived just behind our house and then come back to his bed.

Sometimes a dog has a personality that enables it to help other animals. I had a very special German Shepherd dog that I called Flash, after my first dog, and he could calm other dogs. He was one of a litter of puppies in Inverness that we were asked to take for homing. We got all the puppies except one which the owner planned to sell to someone who wanted a security dog. For some reason, I wanted that particular puppy and I really, really wanted it so much. Not being able to have it just made it worse! I had been telling a friend of ours about this puppy and how much I wanted it. He went down to Inverness and offered the owner money there and then and he arrived here with the puppy who sat beside him looking very aloof. He was an absolute darling: he went everywhere with me and he had a talent for helping me with really difficult dogs.

I have seen the police come in here at 2am with a really terrified dog in the back of their van after a drugs raid. The dog was possibly also high on drugs and definitely not wanting to get out of the van until Flash got in and sat quietly in the corner with it. Then I was able to get a lead onto it and Flash walked with it into the kennels. There was one night we got a call to say there was a stray dog inside a tattie shed on the Black Isle and nobody could get near it, so would I go up there. As I went up one row of tattie boxes, the dog would go down another row. Flash came in and just found the dog. He had a very soothing, calming effect on animals and it was just as if he was telling the wee dog to calm down and everything would be all right. I was able to put a lead on the dog and bring him back here.

Flash could calm other dogs, including one of my own called Bobby who was a bossy, noisy wee thing who could bark in the car all the way to Glasgow. He was a Staffie/cross who came to me as a one-day-old puppy after his mother died giving birth. Flash would place his paw on top of Bobby's head and gently push him down and for thirty seconds or so he would keep Bobby in place until Bobby kind of said "All right, you win. I'm calm."

There were two occasions when Flash calmed a human down as well. A man came in to collect a dog that belonged to him but had been collected as a stray and the owner was really giving a lot of verbal abuse. He was shouting and swearing and waving his arms about when Flash decided to take hold of his arm and hold it, not bite it, but it certainly calmed the chap down. On the second occasion a young chap was really giving me the verbals when Flash jumped up and put a paw on each shoulder. The chap was terrified and I told Flash to get down but told the young man that if he stopped giving me grief, then the dog would not give him grief.

The amazing Flash.

The chap retreated then to his car where his three mates were waiting for him and he made one of them come up to the kennel to retrieve his dog from me and Flash!

Flash surprised most people, and me the first time I saw it, by actually playing with sheep. He would jump over the gate into their field and then, playfully, run at a sheep that would then run at Flash, chasing him round the field. He would then turn and chase the sheep, all in good spirit. I never knew Flash to do anything bad in his life.

Sometimes, I have to fight a battle for an animal. One dog, a wee mongrel, had bitten and when it went to court, the sheriff decided the dog should be put down and a destruction order was put in place. We had been caring for the dog for a few weeks before this came to court and I had got to know the animal. I just knew it would be wrong to do this and so I sent what I can only call a begging letter to the court saying how lovely the dog was, how well behaved and how easy to manage. I explained that he would not be difficult to rehome, so would they please reconsider. They did overturn the ruling and even the solicitors involved were pleased that this animal was not going to be put down. Everyone knew

Dogs come in a variety of shapes and sizes as well as different personalities.

that what had happened was not the dog's fault.

Animals like routine and in here they have that. They hear other dogs barking but not in an unhappy, stressed way and they do not hear people shouting, laughing definitely, but no angry shouting. We have a dog at the moment that came in following a major disturbance and we had to be very wary of him. But, after two weeks he is a different dog. He is happy, playful, eating, enjoying company and responding to the atmosphere in the kennel block. If he does not have to be destroyed by court order, and if his original owners cannot take him back, then we would eventually try to rehome him with the right owner. It would need to be someone used to big strong dogs and who had a quiet, calm manner with a stable lifestyle, who knows and loves that breed and wants to keep the reputation of that breed.

Chapter 7

Finding Homes

Some animals are easier to rehome than others. Cats, for example, are easier to rehome than dogs. Obviously, a dog with a friendly outgoing attitude is more likely to get a home quickly but so is a dog with a really cute face. This is silly because a dog might not be the prettiest - it might be really ugly - but it might have the loveliest personality. Eventually, someone comes along and says the animal is so ugly that it is cute and that is the one they want! Between June 2017 and June 2018 we managed to find homes for 354 dogs and 90 cats.

When rehoming, we do our best to ensure that we match the animal to the potential owner. This is based on information we have been given by a previous owner and the potential owner's circumstances and wishes. I would say as much as 25% of dog rehomings fail but cats are rarely returned. With the returned dogs it is most likely that they have been mismanaged in a previous home and the new owners cannot get them out of that pattern. Maybe they discover that the new animal and their existing pets just do not hit it off. Sometimes a problem develops in relation to children.

Sometimes people choose an animal that is possibly not suited to them. For example, if we have a big strong dog and the person who wants to rehome him does not look like they could physically control the dog then, tactfully, I would question how they were going to exercise him. Perhaps, I would let them get a feel for the dog and try a wee walk which would, hopefully, help them to realise the strength of an animal like that. Once he had jumped up at them and pulled them around for a while, the dog would probably have put them off all by himself! I would maybe try to introduce them to some of the other dogs we have and hopefully, they would fall for a different one that was more suited to them.

I tend to take my time over deciding where any animal goes to. I have to be certain in my mind that the rehoming stands a reasonable chance of success. If it fails, the animal will come back here and, once again, this does no good to the animal, nor to the reputation of Munlochy Animal Aid and may put the people off taking another animal from us.

When someone wants to rehome a dog from us we do not always need to do a home check. For instance, some people have rehomed from us before and might be on their fourth or fifth animal from here or the person is known to us. But we have a small team of people who do home visits for us. They are looking at the appropriateness of the home for the type of animal the people want to rehome. This includes the security offered within the garden and, if they have other animals, the cleanliness of the place with regard to left around poo, which is always a telling sign. You are looking to get an idea of how these folk live and see what they might be offering the animal.

We talk to potential owners about the costs they can anticipate in taking on their chosen animal. We take up veterinarian references, asking the potential owner to get a letter from their vet confirming that they are responsible owners who inoculate, worm, treat health issues and so on because I cannot phone the vet to ask for a reference due to data protection issues.

We need to know that the animal, a dog for example, is likely to get along with whatever other pets the potential owner has. To this end, we 'cat test' the dogs to see how they respond to feline friends. On one occasion, a couple wanted to take a particular dog and asked if we knew whether she could get along with their cat. To 'cat test' we use our own cats who are all very laid back around dogs, living with so many on a daily basis. On this occasion, watched by the potential dog owners, one of our cats wandered past and the dog nearly ripped the lead out of my hand, managing to seriously rip my fingernail in the process. With blood all over my hand, the potential dog owner asked if I thought the dog would be all right with their cat!

Emma with Meg (centre) and their two new pals, Mipsi and Coco.

Feral Tilly Trotter with her kittens. The kittens were for rehoming but Tilly stayed in our house as one of our ever increasing family.

One of our own dogs was a definite cat killer and we had to be very firm with him from the moment he came into our home. He had to become one of the team, which consists of us humans and the cats and dogs. Graham and I were very firm with him and consistent. He would be told to lie down and to stay and he knew by the tone of our voices that we meant business. We never raise our hands to an animal but when we use our voices, they definitely know what will and will not be accepted. The cats can always get height, which I think is a good thing because the cat is higher up than the dog and the window is always open, so they could get out if they want to. We never left him in the room with the cats but he was somewhat thrown by the fact that our cats were not frightened of him and he only had experience of cats that were scared. He is so good with cats now that the new cat that has joined our home will actually walk past him and slap him in the face. His expression is, "What did I do?" This particular dog had a number of issues when he came to stay with us and it took about a year to sort him out. But, he has accepted his place. He knows the cats are very important in this house and he just does not try it on at all. It took a long time before I would trust him enough for me to go out of the room and leave him with the cats but that is what you have to do. It all takes time.

Many rescue dogs have their little issues but you take them, warts and all, and generally speaking, if you give them a couple of months to settle, they can be managed. Sometimes that just is not possible and we always take them back if a rehoming fails. We do live in a world where some people want everything just perfect. If you get an animal that has issues, you get a lot of satisfaction from persevering and, down the line, knowing that you have been able to make a difference to the betterment of both yourself and the animal.

I got a call from the police one night to say a chap had been arrested for drunk driving and although they had got the car to the police station yard, the dog in the back was not about to get out. The dog was very definite about this and making it very clear! So, they asked if I could attend. I realised this was not going to be easy when none of the police offered to come out and help and would only watch from the window. At the time, I still had my beautiful German Shepherd dog called Flash and he was amazing when it came to helping to deal with other dogs. With Flash's help, I got this dog into the cage and then the policemen helped me lift it into the back of my car. I brought him back here and parked as close as I could get to the kennel block and my cousin came to help me get the cage out, open the door and get the dog into the kennel. The

Robbie, who hated cats, with his new pal Topsy!

animal was really furious and was not taking prisoners! When his owner came out from quite a long spell in prison, he left the dog with us and went down south. So now we needed a home for this really difficult dog who we could not yet even take out for a walk. Although we worked hard on him for a long time, he improved a bit but was going to be really difficult to rehome and would have had to stay with us for a very long time before he was ready. Then one day a chap arrived and it was an instant thing between the man and the dog. I could actually see an instant bond between them. He got a lead on the dog, took him for a walk and the dog was as calm as could be. They lived happily together for many years.

I have seen this sudden affinity between a person and an animal on a number of occasions. We had a wee Labrador/cross dog in the kennel and it was absolutely petrified. It was terrified of everything and in those circumstances you sometimes need to back off and just give it time. A family came in to look around and the woman chose this one. I explained that it was a very, very nervous dog and needed more time to settle but she was adamant that it was the dog she wanted. I took the dog out of the pen and, instantly, he adored her as much as she did him. There was an immediate rapport between the two them and it was lovely to see. The dog was so relaxed and comfortable with her and the whole thing worked a treat. The dog got a lovely family and the family got a lovely dog. My own sister, Alexis took an immediate liking to a black Labrador/cross that she called Molly and she is very rarely seen without Molly by her side. It seems that there is definitely an affinity at times and we do not fully understand it but sometimes it is between two people and sometimes between a person and an animal.

Sometimes I can see the fire in an animal's eyes. I always have to think that if I rehome a dog that I know has the potential to attack, and it does attack, then I am doing damage to the reputation of MAA and to the detriment of other dogs, especially those of that same breed. I know it might sound like a touch of arrogance to say it, but it would do my reputation no good either because it is a whole package. People need to feel that they can trust a dog that, as far as I am aware, is not a threat to them or their children, grandchildren or other pets. I am as honest as I can be based upon what I know of the dog's past and the behaviour we have seen whilst it has been in the centre. Sometimes, for both human and animal good, we have to make a decision we would rather not make.

However, 75% of our rehomings result in forever homes. One case in point was Rusty, a wee terrier crossbreed who found his forever home six years ago. Joan and Craig describe their experience with this little character:

"People often ask us 'What kind of dog is that?' Quite honestly, we don't know. Rusty didn't come with documentation on his pedigree, family lineage or guarantees of being well bred. Our dog Rusty came from Munlochy Animal Aid as a playful character, full of beans and unbelievably cute. He is the archetypical mongrel dog; a mixture of Border terrier, long-haired Jack Russell and who knows what else, but with a fantastic and friendly nature.

"We named him Rusty as he epitomises the stereotype of the 'wee ginger dug'. He is the colour of autumn and when we first set eyes on him nearly six-and-a-half years ago it really was a case of love at first sight! Having not had a dog for a couple of years, something was missing in our lives. Purely by chance, I was handing in money collected by a friend to Munlochy Animal Aid and asked if they had any small dogs in needing a home. I was told

50

Rusty enjoying the sunshine in his new forever home.

that Iona would give me a call as there was one wee dog who had only just arrived at the kennels. Iona phoned me later that night and said 'Joan, I can't even describe this dog, just come over in the morning and you will see how great he is!'

"Iona was spot on. We arrived at the kennels early the next morning and were greeted by an absolutely gorgeous wee ginger dog who was desperate to take us for a walk in the nearby forest. We were smitten and Iona suggested that we take him on a month's trial. She did not elaborate on where he had come from or why anybody would have abandoned such a brilliant little character but she felt that when we really got to know him, we would offer him a place in our home.

"In the early days, it was not plain sailing. Whoever had owned this seven-month-old dog had not put any work into training him. In the first few days there were many puddles and damp cloths but he soon got the hang of it. We soon knew that he would fit in just fine with us and to this day we can't believe how lucky we are that Munlochy Animal Aid brought us together.

"Rusty has given us so much in the last six years and, now our children have flown the nest, he has become our daily priority. Walks, company, friendship and much love. We really couldn't imagine life without him."

Chapter 8

Wildcats

It all started when I was driving down Strathconon in late autumn. I arrived at a house to collect a large Jack Russell who, through no fault of his own, needed a new home. Whilst his soon to become ex-owners hunted out his meagre belongings I noticed on the mantelpiece a photograph of a large wildcat, albeit dead, but an unmarked victim of a car. I was absolutely fascinated by the size and beauty of the dead animal and driving back home I thought of little else but the wildcat.

I had a desperate wish to see, first-hand, a living example of this ferocious and independent animal. I just wanted to touch a wildcat - not to trap or tame it - just to have the joy of touching a wildcat. Many years passed before I realised the dream and to date I have enjoyed this experience twice.

The first occasion arose when a couple who lived locally had been lucky enough to know of the existence of a wildcat and her kitten and had been watching developments with great interest, from a distance. So after the mother was run over they arrived on my doorstep with this furry little kitten. It was bitterly cold weather and the kitten was very poorly. He slept the night on top of me under the bedclothes in order to thaw out. By the next day there was some improvement. He slept in the same place for the second night. But, once thawed, he came to life and I had a wee terrorist on my hands. He was just a bundle of fury. I telephoned a friend and told him what I had, so he came to see him. There was this tiny kitten sitting on top of the fridge-freezer hissing and spitting at him. The wildcat definitely did not want to be touched. I kept the kitten for a wee while and during that time he got a really good

The pussycat made it very clear he did not want to be stroked!

health check and inoculated. Eventually, after taking advice from experts, we slowly released this ferocious pussycat into a safe area.

On the second occasion, a Minister from Muir of Ord brought me a tiny wee kitten whose mother had also been killed by a car. He was only about four weeks old and was much too small to go in with the other cats, so I put him in my bedroom and went to get a dish of food for him. When I went back into the room with it he was nowhere to be seen. Frantically, I searched under the bed, in the bedside cabinet, everywhere but could not find him. I sat on the bed just stunned because I had lost this tiny four-week-old creature. I repeated the searching and then I heard a strange sound coming from my recently folded laundry pile in the corner. Sure enough, there he was tucked up very nicely in the midst of my underwear! He enjoyed the food I offered him. Very quickly he showed an interest in my beautiful grey male cat called Barnie. The two became devoted to each other and I was overjoyed.

After a few days I let him out, always anxious that even though he was only a kitten he might vanish. But, no, he enjoyed his comfort and slept on my bed with Barnie and Mr Scruffy, my beloved dog. As he grew, he became Mr Scruffy's shadow. They got on so well together that he would often be found sound asleep on Mr Scruffy's back. Tiger, as he was called, began to come out walking with myself and the three dogs. They were a very happy bunch and, of course, I was in my element since I was touching a wildcat every day! Tiger had to have his inoculations and I took our vet's advice to have him neutered.

As Tiger grew, I tried to give him a touch of normal wildcat diet when a local gamekeeper, who was trying to control the rabbit population, offered me one of his victims. Although I am a vegetarian and would never kill any creature, I decided to accept the gift of a rabbit. Suddenly this lovely docile seventeen-weekold kitten changed into a wild little savage. He grabbed the rabbit, running off into the bushes and any approach from me or any of his animal friends brought forth a very hostile reaction. A couple of hours later, as I went into the bathroom, here was Tiger and his booty in the bottom of the airing cupboard. He had eaten the head and was into the shoulders! I could not believe the strength in his jaws. Nothing would part him from his rabbit, which he ate completely but he never got another little body to take into my airing cupboard.

Obviously, we had to worm Tiger just as we do the other cats but he was not easily fooled. While the other cats scoffed their food with pills hidden inside, Tiger could tell instantly and he would refuse all offers, however tasty. He would even turn down his favourite, which was chicken. Eventually, we managed it by combining chicken with the most expensive wormers on the market!

His love of chicken knew no bounds. One Christmas a friend gave me a cooked chicken as a gift for my cats. Since it was still hot, I had to hide the chicken and decided to stash it in my bedroom. I know that seems a strange place to put a chicken but my cats were crazy about the stuff and I thought it would be safe until I could chop it up. However, Tiger had other plans and managed to sneak unseen into the bedroom. He was about six months old now and enjoyed fairly large meals. He clearly enjoyed a feast that day, devouring half the chicken, crunching the bones as they got in his way. When I eventually found him he was hidden inside my nightdress with only his head sticking out. He was so full I do not

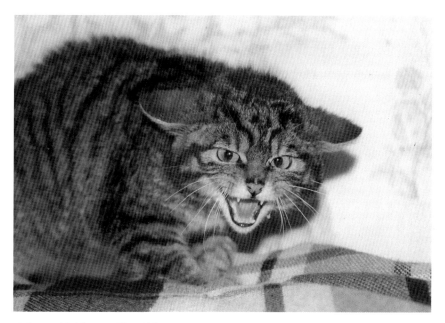

A beautiful but still wild creature.

think he could have moved.

The time came when I could see a change in Tiger. He started to parade around almost like a caged animal. He had never been locked up and was free to come and go as he pleased. But it was as if he was in a mental cage. He was becoming very unsettled and moved around the house more and more. I was very worried and I had every reason to be since one day he went out and we never saw him again. I was devastated. I walked for miles day after day with Mr Scruffy, calling his name. Mr Scruffy would look hopefully around but there was no sign of Tiger. Tiger, the wildcat, had made his choice. I am sure that the natural instinct never left him and the call of the wild won in the end. Poor Mr. Scruffy had lost his friend.

Chapter 9

Goats and Sheep

Over the years we have probably had eight or so goats. We have never had them for milking or breeding and a lot of them have come from out on the hills. Slioch, as I called him, was probably only two days old when he was brought in. A chap was out walking on a Sunday afternoon in March up behind Loch Maree and a storm started. When he began the walk he saw this wee goat by itself and he thought that was a bit strange. It was still there when he returned, by which time the snow storm was much worse, so he knew he could not just leave the wee thing. He phoned and said could he bring in this tiny, soaked, cold and hungry little goat. We did not have goats milk so we used lambs milk to feed it, keeping it warm in the utility room where there is a tiled floor and heating because the weather was really cold. Slioch took to the bottle easily and would follow Graham and me around the place. He grew so quickly that in a couple of weeks we decided he was going out. He was jumping into the sink and I knew he would be up on top of the tumble dryer next, so out he had to go.

We made a pen for him, on his own at first, and then he was introduced to the sheep. At night we would shut him in with the rabbits because we shut all our animals in overnight: you never know what will come in at night, so they keep safe. He had to be castrated as young as possible and reluctantly we let the vet take the horns off. They make such handsome animals with their horns on but it is safer and I don't regret it now. Slioch is a mischievous load of fun!

There are wild goats roaming around outside Golspie. A couple of them had been going into gardens and onto the main road

Slioch - butter would not melt in his mouth, but it would sizzle!

where one of them was eventually killed. I got a telephone call asking if I would take a goat that is really wild as the heather. The people had managed to get him cornered and the only escape for him was onto a float so that was how they brought him in. I called this young goat Bhraggie.

Normally, we introduce animals slowly but with him we just had to open the float and let him get on with it. Luckily, he made himself at home very quickly but never tamed down like Slioch. When animals arrive and see other animals so relaxed and they realise they are getting fed twice a day around the same time and everything is consistent, they settle down. He had no stress and nobody pushing him to do anything. We did, however, have to catch him and sedate him to be castrated but we left the horns on and this did concern me because even a neutered billy can get quite aggressive as they get older. He was a gorgeous, stunning looking beast and went from coat hanger thin to the magnificent animal he became. Unfortunately, Bhraggie developed crippling arthritis in his front legs that was not treatable and so he had to be put down.

We have had rescue sheep and orphaned lambs for a number of years. We have taken sheep when someone passes away or when they are taken in a cruelty case. Sometimes, we bought sheep that were in a poor condition in order to rescue them.

Our first four needed a lot of attention but they tamed down nicely and were really friendly. Although they were shut in at night for safety, the place was not that well fenced when they came and they would roam the field and go down to my sister's and over to the cottages. One morning I got a call from the police asking if we were missing four sheep who were down munching grass on the side of the A9 down near Kessock junction. Fortunately, I was friendly with the local bobby and his wife and he picked me up with a bucket of food. He dropped me off and the sheep walked all the way back with me. Kindly, he reversed back to the junction with his blue light flashing but it was amazing that the cars did not slow down. Surely, if you see animals on the road and a police car lights flashing you would slow down but, that day, they did not. They all got back safe and sound and after that the place was fenced properly.

I found a sheep once at the side of the road with its udder burst and I took it home and called the vet. He took a look and said I was not going to win with this but I explained that I was going to give it a try. We called her Belle and she had the vet here for her first ten days on the trot but managed to live to a ripe old age. One of our current sheep, Bonnie Morag adores custard creams and ginger nuts and will come running for them.

Who could resist these two wee rascals?

"Who do you think you're looking at?"

Chapter 10

Otters and Seals

We have had good success with wild creatures like the otters and seals. It is quite strange that when you get young otters or seals the commonest cause is the bad weather. It has often been the case that there has been horrific snow.

For example, the last seal that we had needed to stay with us for a couple of months because the weather was so bad that it was just too dangerous to try to make the journey down south to the SSPCA wildlife centre and they could not get up north to us. So, we turned one of our isolation pens into a wet room. I had to make raw fish soup, which is disgusting, and Graham had to wear welders gauntlets to prise the jaws open of this young seal so that we could tube feed him. It was really hard work and no sooner had you finished one feed than you had to start all over again. The whole place smelt of fish. When I went to sleep it was to the smell of fish and when I awoke it was to fish. It was worth it though to see the change in this wee creature that came in with sunken eyes and loose skin, a sign that he had been suffering for some time. We did get him down to Fishcross, the SSPCA Wildlife Centre, but we never heard what happened to him so we assume he stayed until he was ready to go out into the sea with the other seals. It is wonderful to be able to give these wild creatures another chance at life.

Having baby otters was a fabulous experience. They are so cute that you want to cuddle them but we try to minimize human contact. They are going back to the wild and you have got to keep them wild, if at all possible. The first time, mum and I were driving past a bar on the river in Inverness and stopped at the traffic lights. In those days, everyone knew our van and they came out from the bar thinking we had arrived for the baby otters who had come into the bar, totally lost. There was nothing we could do but just take them home with us and start on all the hard work, but what a fabulous experience. They could eat for themselves if you gave them the fish but they were tiny babies. I gave them a bowl of water big enough for them to climb in and out and splash around. I used to sing to them when they were tired and it would send them off to sleep: The Mingulay Boat Song was their favourite. The newspaper had printed an article about them and I had jokingly said that I could not remember all the words of that song. Loads of people then contacted me, sending me the words. It had been a joke because the baby otters did not really care about the words, I could just have hummed it and they liked the sound. Their eyelids would get heavier and they would go off to sleep.

Chapter 11

Pigs

We have had different types of pigs. Our first pig was mentioned in conversation by an SSPCA inspector who wondered if I could take it. It was a wee pot-bellied pig and I thought it was a lovely idea, having a wee pig, since we have quite a lot of ground. When I told my mother that I had said 'yes' to a pig she was far from pleased. She said I had definitely done the wrong thing by saying 'yes'. However, when the inspector arrived with the pig, pulled up to the field and let out this pig, my mother was smitten instantly.

Then an SSPCA inspector asked me one day if I could do him a favour, to which I replied that if I could then I would. He went on to ask could I take another wee pig that was very small and would fit inside a cat box. He did not mention that it would grow into a ton and a half of pink pig! The pig made a break for it one day and took off down the road. Dad's cousin, Isobel, lived along the road and, not being very well at the time, was watching from her bedroom window. She said it was such good fun watching me, on my own, trying to catch a ton and a half of pig. I knew it was never going to happen, so I called my sister and asked her to please slow down any traffic because I knew the school bus was due. Well, it would have been as much good having the cat slow down the traffic because she was so polite about it, just making little hand signals and mouthing the words 'slow down' very quietly. In fact, none of the drivers knew what she was trying to do! Eventually, the pig got a bit bored and went into Isobel's garden. She had a nice garden with flowers and vegetable plot and, over in the corner, she had beehives. This pig did not trample any flowers, just kept running down this path and along that path until she came to

Peggy, our first pig.

the beehives. You could see she was really having fun until she reached the hives, whereupon she slowed right down, walked past the hives and then took off again at speed when she got past them. Maybe it was the smell or the sound of the bees but she knew what she doing. When we eventually got her back she just lay down and slept.

She was great fun but, like most pigs, she made a terrible patient. When she was sick or anything was wrong she was dying, never mind if it was just a damaged nail. One time, we could not work out what was wrong with this pig. The vets came out and gave her injections which caused her to scream loudly. Because of the type of skin a pig has, when you give them an injection some of it inevitably flows back out, so the vet has to modify the dose accordingly. This poorly pig would not eat unless I made her porridge and spooned it into her mouth, whilst she lay on her side, refusing even to sit up to take it. I was worried. Then someone came in holding a Terry's Chocolate Orange which she showed an interest in. When she tasted that, well, she sprang to life and wanted more, and quick. We could find absolutely nothing wrong with her. The only thing we can think is that maybe she was coming into season and it was hormonal but I just do not know. After this episode, she would take a slice of chocolate from your hand so gently and always look for second helpings.

The poor thing had to be put down when she was older because her back legs started to give way like many weighty animals. Let's face it, pigs are not designed for long life and usually have about eight or nine months but she had eight or nine years of really lovely life. Vets really do not like having to put down a pig because it can go disastrously wrong but we were lucky in that the vet that came out was absolutely spot on and the pig just slipped into a peaceful sleep.

We have had a pig that fell of a lorry on the Kessock Bridge but the one we have now fell off a lorry at the Forth Road Bridge. They take them in lorries whilst they are very small and there are gaps at the side of the lorry, so when they stop at a filling station or for a meal break, out comes the pig. She is called Pippa Pig and she will live out her life on the croft. When she first arrived, this wee pig slept in the kennels tucked into a duvet and now she is huge. When she got too big for the kennel Graham had to carry her to the field and she screamed and screamed. Pigs make an awful fuss! She was moved from the kennel into the field behind the kennel and she was having great fun rooting around and basically destroying the field. We decided that we would make a pen for her in the wood area. Pigs can get sunburnt in the summer and cold in the winter so by being in the wood she has shade and shelter. So Graham made a super big area with a pig house in it. Could we get her to leave the field and come out to the new pen? No! She would put one foot on the tarmac and then step back. We tried everything, including trying to put a lead on her and bringing Robbie the German Shepherd dog out to see if he could annoy her enough but no, absolutely nothing would persuade her to leave her field. So, in the end, we laid a path of hay but she would not follow it:

Lucky and Lady waiting patiently for their Christmas treats.

we tempted her with buckets of food but she just put her head down and refused to look at us. We spent most of the day trying to move her and we had something else to do at about 4pm. We were starting to get irritable and Graham said a few words that a pig should never have to hear! So he decided to get her into the container where the sheep and the goats go to eat their hay and if he could get her in there he would then drive up and get her into the float. This manoeuvre worked and so he drove her across the tarmac and reversed the float to her new pen. She refused to come out of the float. Even the other pig, the grumpiest old sow I have ever known, came and pushed her a few times to see if she was still alive but no amount of pushing and poking would move this two-ton pig. So we decided to leave her there, safe until the morning. When we got up she had gone into the pen and she loves it. She loves people to speak to her and to stroke behind her ears. Pippa is always pleased to see you, checking out whether you have a biscuit or an apple for her. When we did a barbecue, including bacon, she was standing watching because she just loves people and being in the middle of everything.

One of our pigs came over on the boat from an island. The owners were people who had come up from the south with the intention of living the good life but without a full understanding of what this involved. Their pig had been shut indoors in an enclosure that had not been cleaned properly so, despite the fact that they are naturally very clean animals, we had to give her a good scrubbing down. She settled in really quickly. I think what did it was just having a good life in a field where she could forage around, having the company of another pig and having proper pig food. She lived a long life. We do give all our animals treats but they also have to have the proper food for their breed.

Chapter 12

Horses

It all started because there were horses down the Longman area and we were aware of a number of them that were in a very bad way. If it was freezing cold and icy, there was no water for them and if it was scorching hot, there was no water. We were constantly back and forth trying to do something for these horses, as were another two or three people, thankfully. We found out who the owners were and we made a relationship with them so that they would accept us getting involved with their horses. What they did not know was that in the background, at the same time, we were harassing the council who owned the ground that the horses were on. We went on at them about a council allowing this cruelty to go on and doing nothing about it.

There was one year when a horse gave birth to her foal in the middle of this muddy field: the foal had died and it just laid there, nobody moving it. This situation, and our commitment, went on for years until one holiday weekend the council struck and issued an eviction notice. The expiry date of the eviction notice was the next Monday, so the owners could do nothing as the council offices were closed. The notice stated that if these horses were not removed by their owners then the council would arrange for their removal and recover the cost by selling the horses, or words to that effect. The owners were furious but they had nowhere to put the horses, so we were able to take them. To get those horses here was such a relief because there just were not enough hours in the day to be going back and forth to Inverness for three years to help these horses each day. We did not have anything in place so we had to house them in the track leading up to my granny's old home and

Dad repaired the roof of the byre so they could get shelter. Eventually, we managed to access more ground and make better shelters for them.

More and more horses have come and we now have eighteen, which is the maximum we can accommodate. One of my nieces, also called Iona, has become very involved with our horses as well as caring for the sheep. When Iona and her sister Eilidh were wee my father took them riding every Sunday and Iona was so confident around the horses. She is in the fields every day, regardless of the weather and up there in the dark to check if they need anything at the end of the day. We have some very fiery, feisty horses but Iona can handle them and seems to have the ability to calm even the most difficult horse. They see Iona and rush up to her to see what she has got for them. To see her handle these animals when, for example, the farrier comes is very impressive. She loves and respects them and they reciprocate.

We do not rehome these horses, so they will remain here for their natural lives. We do not want someone to take a horse and then, after a couple of years, to give it up because it just does not suit their needs any more. Having a horse is so expensive and when people take on a horse or a pony they may not realise the full costs involved.

One of the horses we were asked to take was due to be shot because it was said to be so dangerous. I talked it over with my niece Iona and it was agreed that if it was as dangerous as they said we would have to put it down. I would not endanger her safety nor that of the blacksmith or vet. As it happens, the horse has settled down and lives quietly with the others. We do not ask anything of it and it will never be ridden nor put in a horsebox, unless essential and it will just live out its natural life fed, watered, sheltered and cared for.

A life with no stresses.

Chapter 13

Feathered Friends

We have had all kinds of birds, including raptors. Graham is becoming somewhat of an expert in dealing with raptors. For some reason, he seems to have a natural gift for getting them to eat when the vets cannot. A vet will ring up and ask if there is any chance of us taking a raptor. We currently have two owls, one of which has been here for six years. He has a damaged wing and although he can just fly, he can only fly in a circle so he could not exist out in the wild. He lives within a huge enclosed area with an indoor section where he and the resident buzzards, which are also damaged, can get in if the weather is really rough. If a bird cannot take the normal amount of exercise that they would get in the wild they are more likely to feel the cold, so they need somewhere to get warm. Graham feeds them with chicken or even venison that is given to us. Any extra is given to the buzzards and kites that fly around near the croft.

I have always rescued seagulls and pigeons. I know people call them flying rats but they are beautiful birds, so clean, and to watch them fly is stunning. The first one was a wee chick fallen from a nest and hand reared. The RSPB officer was interested in this bird so he put a ring on it in the hope that people might realise it was tame and not treat it badly. When the bird grew, it would fly away every night and come back the next morning for a meal. And then we would get another seagull and another seagull and over the years I have had so many seagulls passing through that now there is a couple of hundred who turn up looking for a meal. I say they all have family connections! If the winter is really bad we will feed them twice a day so they turn up again in the afternoon but they are clean, healthy, well-fed birds.

On one occasion, I had climbed up Ben Nevis with a cousin, the second time I had done it, and I was worn out, so I sat down and got out my chocolate bar. A lone seagull swooped down right over my head, determined to get my energy-giving chocolate! He did not get it but we did give him something else to eat. That is over 4,000 feet up so that is pretty high for a seagull and I wondered, did he follow me?

We have always had chickens but we were once involved in the rescue of over one thousand chickens from down near Braemar. Somebody had allowed a situation to get out of hand. I have never seen so many chickens in sheds that were falling down. Some of the sheds were only held together with excrement. The SSPCA, Hen Rescue and other organisations took about a thousand chickens between them and we took 231. I had it all organised and I had homes for every one of them except the twelve that I was keeping. They were all old ladies and they were all past their best so nobody was overwhelmed with eggs! Hens are lovely to have but they have their downside. If you are feeding them outside they attract rats which can be a real nuisance.

We have had geese and they were lovely to have around. But, the one we have at the moment, Glen, came from a dog warden who was emigrating to Australia. Whilst I agreed to take Glen, I have regretted it many times since he can be very aggressive and will chase me down the field, slapping me with his wing and pecking me really hard. When Glen's friend, who was a Muscovy duck, died he was left with just the chickens, sheep and goats who share his field but I have decided he is the last goose I am going to take in!

The funniest bird I had was a Little Auk who had probably been windblown but was not terribly poorly. I filled the bath and that was his pond where he would dive for the pieces of fish that I cut up. I asked the RSPB officer where would be the best place to release him. He said it was Chanonry Point and I should just stand him beside the water rather than put him in it. One day, I drove to Chanonry with the Auk in his little box. I emptied him out to stand beside the water and then walked back up to my car. I noticed that

71

Daffy shows off her swimming skills in a basin.

there were a couple sitting in a car laughing their heads off. Now, I knew I probably was dressed a bit oddly and depositing a bird by the water was unusual, but not *that* funny. When I looked behind me, there was the Auk following me up from the water, so I had to put him back in the box and drive him home. We kept him for another wee while in case he just did not feel he was ready to leave. But the next time, I released him at North Kessock and he was off with no trouble.

I was in Inverness one day and was walking through the market when I saw three lads pushing a tiny baby pigeon, still a fluffy yellow ball of down, along the ground. I gathered him up and we reared Percy the Pigeon. He would fly in and out, landing on a cupboard in the kitchen, leaning on one wing as if it was his elbow, while he watched what was going on. When we walked the dogs he would come too, flying up and down over our heads, teasing the dogs, and landing on my shoulder to nibble my ear. Other people did not find it quite so endearing when he landed on them and gave them the playful peck! He was with us for years until old age caught up with him.

Chapter 14

The More Unusual Visitors

There is nothing we would not take but that does not mean they would stay here. We would take anything in as an emergency situation, even rather exotic animals such as snakes and iguanas, but these are only here temporarily until we can pass them on to someone who understands their needs better than we do. If we do not know what to do, then I have been doing this for so long that I probably know someone who does know what to do. I actually have a long list of names of people I can contact to ask what we should do; what is the best and the right thing to do. We try to pass these creatures on to someone better placed to care for them than us.

Iguanas
I had an iguana here once that had been living in a fish tank that was probably about two feet too short for the animal. He was quite literally doubled up all the time with no special heating or the light he needed. I just kept him until I could get someone with an interest and expertise in caring for this kind of animal to take him. As it happened, a friend called Cathy, who was also a vet, had a special interest in reptiles and someone she knew made a wonderful enclosure in the house for the iguana, with all the proper lighting and tree branches. The creature's life just changed and he was there for 19 years.

A Badger
We had a badger that had been hit by a car and had a nasty head injury and various cuts. We made a pen out in a shed for him and

Brock, almost ready for release.

got the vet out to examine him but we did not know whether he would survive. He did and we named him Brock. We kept him for a few weeks until the vet said he was able to be returned to the wild. He was a big lad and ate plenty of dog food while he was with us.

He had never tried to bite me or maul me except the day that the photographer came from the Press and Journal to take a photograph of him. He asked me to stand beside the pen and when I rested my hand on the top of the pen, Brock bit my hand. But it was not a serious bite and certainly not what he could have done. We found out exactly where he had been picked up by the person who had brought him in and that was where we released him late at night, so he was in his own territory. It is a wonderful feeling when you release a wild animal.

You feel kind of sad when they go because they have been safe and protected with us but you feel glad at the same time because they have gone back to their natural environment, but they are on their own.

Squirrel Nutkin stuffing his face, as usual.

Squirrels

A forestry worker presented us with two baby squirrels that had come down with the dray when a tree was felled. There was no sign of the mother but these two squirrels were about the size of my little finger. They were completely hairless, eyes shut and absolutely crawling with fleas. At that size they could not possibly have the usual flea control so I used a herbal one and the fleas just ran off them. I wrapped a hot water bottle and laid them on it to warm them up. For very small animals I feed them on cotton buds. I soaked the buds in the milk we use for kittens and let them suck on it as if they were drinking from their mother. They did amazingly well, staying in a big fish tank with their hot water bottle so they were free of draughts. They enjoyed fruit, nuts and fir cones and, in particular, they loved custard cream biscuits, opening them up to lick the cream in the middle.

I had to keep them for about eight months until it was the right time of the year to release them and they were of an age to survive alone. They had a big cage and in it I put an old handbag which they used as their bed. As they grew and thrived they became extremely active, flying, not jumping around the house, from the curtain rail to the dog's back and onto the chair. In late spring we took the cage out and did what I consider a slow release. This involves leaving them in the cage just to get used to the great outdoors but bringing them in at night. Then, they are left out at night with the cage closed until I open it in the morning.

Eventually, the squirrels just went off together into the wood. I left the cage there for a long time with the door open and food inside but I do not know what ate the food, so it could have been them or something else. We currently have four feeding stations for squirrels and there is a colony of them in the wood.

Mice

The soaked cotton bud came into use again when Graham inadvertently killed a mouse when moving our shed and then discovered that there was a nest with two very, very wee baby mice in it. He felt awful since it was just a couple of days before Christmas and he had killed their mother. They remained with us in a super big tank with bits to climb on and hide in and there they stayed until they died when they were two-and-a-half years old. My own cats would just watch them but were never left alone in the same room with them.

Deer

We have had fawns in the house. Some have been abandoned and some have come in after their mother has been killed by a car. I had one fawn that was just days old when it was brought in with a broken leg. She had her leg splinted and was adopted by one of our particularly gentle dogs. They would lie beside each other, the fawn getting warmth from her. She was bottle fed and would then sleep for hours, so much easier than feeding a puppy or kitten. They tame very easily but I never take in a wild animal with the intention of keeping it as a pet. They belong in the wild unless a vet says that, for whatever reason, they cannot be released. She would skip around the house, passing urine as she went and then laying down in the front garden. She would go in and out of the field with the sheep and goats until she got big and then one day

"Ain't I just too cute for words?"

she just jumped the fence and was gone. She would have been ready for release quite soon because you can see when the call of the wild is becoming stronger in them but she chose when to go. However, she would go down to my friend Margaret's house every night for digestive biscuits and up to another person's house to watch him groom his dog.

Foxes

We have had foxes brought in by members of the public and, sadly, the last two were fitting when they came in and the vet thought they had been poisoned, so they had to be put to sleep. I had a fox cub once which got on really well with our dogs but he was never locked up and came and went as he wanted until one day he just left. He was ready.

The Stoat

We have even had a baby stoat that was picked up when its mother was crossing the road with the other young ones and left this one behind in the road. It was hand reared and the press got to hear about this so came up to take photographs. Holding the stoat for a photo was like holding water and it got down, only to run immediately straight up Graham's trouser leg. Again we did a slow release with our stoat. He came back each day to the cage to eat his food but after a while he was off on his own. However, one of the dog walkers believes that she saw him because a stoat stood up in front of her and the dog she was walking and just stared at them before going off into the undergrowth. He was clearly used to humans and dogs.

Rabbits and Guinea Pigs

In the good weather, rabbits and guinea pigs can live outside in pens but when it is too cold they come into one of the sheds or the reception chalet. Far from being disturbed by all the comings and goings in reception, they seem to enjoy watching everything, listening intently to all the conversations and getting a huge amount of attention from everyone. They get to see and hear all sorts of animals that, from time to time, join them in the reception chalet, from parrots to mice, from cats to poorly chickens and the occasional hedgehog.

Rodney checking out the side salad.

Peter Rabbit.

Chapter 15

Helping Hands

Throughout this book I have paid tribute to the help given to MAA by so many people. If I were to mention every person who has helped us over the forty years of our existence, and every way in which they have helped us, this book would be as long as *War and Peace*! They all have my undying gratitude. Family have always been there, doing whatever they could and for the past eleven years, Graham, my husband, who has made such a wonderful difference to my life, has become more and more important to the running of MAA.

There are so many people who are not relatives but who choose to help just because they love animals. There are those who sit for hours, often freezing, with collecting tins; those who collect food donations left in supermarkets and manage our bookstall; those who run stalls at car boot sales and in village halls; those who bake and sell cupcakes and, of course, Moira's famous lemon drizzle cake; companies that donate valuable prizes for our raffles; and those members of the public who call in with donations of food, bedding, and money. Some folk help in less direct hands-on ways, publicizing what we do, wishing us well in our endeavours or leaving legacies.

One of the ways in which our volunteers help is by coming, in all weathers, to walk dogs. We currently have about twenty-five volunteers who walk dogs, some coming every day and some once a week. The difference these people make to the lives of these dogs and to the people working here is unimaginable. It can also take a bit of pressure off the staff because they know the dogs are getting proper walks and one-to-one attention.

The first volunteer, Susan, was working in Inverness but used to come in her lunch break to walk dogs. Then Susan brought her husband Jamie along to help. To this day, they still walk dogs three or four times a week, run tombola stalls and car boot sales and tirelessly promote our work. Then someone called Margaret moved into one of our properties close by and, although she was working, she would walk dogs while I cleaned their pens. When she had a holiday and at weekends she would help and we formed a good and lasting friendship. She gradually became more and more involved and she is just so important to this place.

I want the volunteers to get something out of the experience themselves. It is a sociable thing, everyone is friendly, and it is a nice atmosphere and we try to make volunteering pleasant for everyone. Of course, being around animals is an amazing experience. When someone comes along saying they would like to join the dog walkers I interview them and I pick up a feeling about their general attitude, how practical they will be, and how much common sense they seem to have. There have been very few people who have asked to volunteer and I have felt the need to reject their offer. We have a huge amount of work to do each day and everyone who volunteers here has got to be able to play their part, get along with each other and not need nursing along all the time.

We also have youngsters who want to volunteer and so long as they are fourteen or over they can join us, but, sometimes, I have told them to come back in six months or so because they are just not ready. Some of the youngsters are on Duke of Edinburgh Awards Scheme, others on work experience and some just wanting to help around animals. They have to work while they are here and it is not just a 'jolly'. I have to know that any volunteer is not going to be a hindrance to us or the staff working here every day.

I would like to use this chapter to give an insight into some of the things our volunteer dog walkers get up to.

Derek

Derek started walking dogs at MAA in March 2004. It was not until 2009 that he got his own home and was able to adopt a beautiful Collie/cross called Fudge. Poor Fudge had been badly treated and was hard work but well worth the effort. Derek realised she had decided to trust him when she was able to go into such a deep sleep that she would snore, loudly. Fudge and Derek were together for three years before she died. He claims that Graham and I decided he needed another dog and so a massive Greyhound called Charlie (racing name Light of Foot) came into his life. For the first year, Charlie had to be muzzled when off his lead since he would attack small dogs. The three wee ones he regularly met would growl as soon as they saw him but eventually, he and they became the best of pals. Charlie, in Derek's words, 'went over the rainbow bridge' after five years living with him. Derek now has a brown/blue Whippet called Emily who sleeps under his duvet since she dislikes the cold. In Derek's own words: "I have made many good friends, two- and four-legged, at MAA and have thoroughly enjoyed my time there. Iona thinks she is lucky to have so many volunteers: I think the volunteers are the lucky ones since we get so much out of it!"

Willie and Heather

Willie and Heather used to live in Tain and Heather would come to Munlochy around Christmas to bring treats for the dogs. In the Christmas of 1995 she saw a poor-looking Lurcher sitting in my Landrover. He had apparently been tied up outside the gates the previous night and had, amongst other injuries, a bad case of mange requiring numerous baths. Heather could not get the Lurcher out of her mind and by February Whisky had joined them and their other dog in his forever home.

Heather started walking dogs each week, cleaning out kennels, fundraising, knitting blanket squares, making dog beds out of old duvets. When Willie retired he started dog walking and later doing the book-keeping. He likes to emphasize that this was in a big book, no computer, and with the grand sum of ú200 in the bank account. Heather says her nickname is 'the sewer executive' because she always ends up scooping poop after her walking duties. They say whatever they are doing it is fun and they do it because they love animals. But they also enjoy the social side of it: a bit of banter over a cuppa with other walkers. They have become trustees of the charity.

Many of their dogs have come from MAA. Willie even brought

home one of their Lurchers on Christmas day, decorated with tinsel, as a surprise for Heather! They have fostered a number of dogs, usually elderly ones that would be too distressed by kennel life or those who are recovering from an operation. One was so skinny they had to walk it with a coat on just to cover it up. However, despite taking dogs for 'a couple of weeks' they often end up with them living out their lives with them. They fostered one poorly elderly dog for eighteen months, taking it to visit its elderly owner in hospital and to see her when she was dying.

Despite regularly saying they are having no more dogs, they do. At the moment they have a Lurcher who was found in a car park near Ben Nevis. It had a major leg injury and MAA agreed to pay for the operation it needed. Recovering in the kennel block was difficult so Willie, who says the dog was looking at him, took it home with no prior discussion with Heather. It is a paragon of virtue, except it will steal Willie's underpants and socks from their bedroom! Willie and Heather have walked dogs for over twenty years and they feel that they are putting their free time to very good use.

Lyn and Ian

Lyn and Ian's association with MAA started 17 years ago when Lyn agreed to help out at a fundraising collection. Then, both Lyn and Ian began dog walking on Sunday mornings. In 2012, dog rehoming had slowed down and Ian suggested a Facebook page as a shop window for dogs looking for homes, with a photo and a few lines of text about each dog. This resulted in dozens of people wanting to adopt these dogs, but without necessarily having thought through the implications of taking one of them on. Sorting through all the applications took up so much time that Ian and I decided to stop using it for this purpose. The Facebook page is now used to alert people to missing pets, put up photos, answer queries and make announcements and has attracted 16,000 followers.

When a couple who had been running a bookstall for Guide Dogs for the Blind in Telford Street Co-op decided to retire, they contacted me to see if MAA would be interested in taking this over. Lyn and Ian have run this for the last four years. They go in every morning, tidying and replenishing the books which sell at 50p each. Between forty and fifty are sold each day, bringing in over ú100 per week which is a great help. Ian prints around 200 Christmas cards for MAA and Lyn continues with her fundraising.

Ian says: "All in all, we are kept pretty busy in our old age. Just sometimes - like yesterday when I answered fourteen messages on FB or some mornings when we arrive at the Co-op to find the mess our bookstall is in - we can't wait for retirement!"

Chris

Chris found out about MAA from my cousin and since then has had four dogs, two Collies and two Spaniels from the kennels, his first Collie staying with him for fifteen years. Initially, Chris was walking dogs on the weekends and would sometimes take a dog away with him for a break in his caravan. Now he is retired, he is able to walk dogs most days and that has gradually turned into him doing a few other tasks around the place. Chris enjoys being around MAA, saying that it gets him out of the house. He thoroughly enjoys the banter with other animal-lovers and will never live down the day that he was gone so long walking with a dog that we were getting ready to send out a search party. I can leave it to the reader to wonder why Chris is also known as 'Del Boy'!

Angie

Angie started her relationship with MAA in 2012 when, on her first day of volunteering, she was presented with a very large German Shepherd, by the name of Candy, to take for a walk. Her heart was pounding because, growing up on army estates it was the preferred breed of dog at the time and they used to run in packs, so she had a fear of GSDs. After walking this loving lady dog, her fear had diminished. She has had two dogs from MAA, both quirky but then Angie says that she is quirky as well!

We have fun at the kennels. One day, after walking a very large Staffordshire Bull Terrier Angie returned him to his pen, took off his lead and attempted to leave. He, however, decided that he wanted to share his love with her leg and, having one hand on the kennel door, she tried with the other hand to pull him off. This simply excited him more and her trousers started to come down,

Part of the feral cats' outdoor playground.

so with her free hand she hung on to her breeks. When Angie shouted for help, another volunteer appeared only to stand having a good giggle before enticing the dog off.

Angie says Graham and I have never declined to help any of the many animals she has presented us with: baby voles, crows, seagulls and what she thought was a woodpecker, but it turned out to be a pigeon, have all come to MAA. A couple of years ago, somebody dumped two baby bantam cockerels on Dava Moor and I said MAA would take them if Angie could catch them. Angie fed them for two months in the hope of catching them. One of them got run over but the loan of two lady chickens was needed to lure the remaining cockerel into a crate. It worked and Angie was ecstatic but the cockerel was not! He has cheered up now that we have got him two French Bantam ladies of his own to live with.

Peter and Ruth
Peter and Ruth had been helping out in an animal sanctuary overseas before they moved back to Scotland in 2010. Since then, they

have walked dogs for at least two hours almost every morning. They will sometimes check out a prospective new home for one of our dogs and are always willing to do various fundraising activities.

Peter says walking dogs is a great way to keep fit and they enjoy the company of both the dogs and the other volunteers and staff. Their own dog, a Lurcher called Colin, came to them 'just for a few days' for some kennel stress respite while his tailectomy healed over six years ago! There is usually at least one dog in the kennel that Colin will walk with, so he generally shares his first walk of the day in the company of a kennel dog. Peter and Ruth took Colin and a little Shitsu along to a care home but Colin was pretty freaked out and spent the whole time trying to leave. The little Shitsu on the other hand behaved quite well, despite being suddenly grabbed by the ears and kissed on the nose. However, neither got invited back.

Peter often walks the bigger and more difficult dogs and it gives him a great sense of achievement when they settle down to a more normal state and especially when they go to a forever home. It is wonderful to watch Peter walking one of these big, strong dogs beside Ruth who might be walking a wee pug and a poodle. He played a big part in helping a couple of the more difficult GSDs by building up a relationship with them. This included doing 'magic' tricks with their favourite ball. This involved slowly lifting the ball up and over his head and out of sight, dropping it into his hood before showing them his now empty hands. The big, older male GSD would search round and round his feet but the bitch, who was perhaps more intelligent, would look at him for a moment before running off searching downhill because it just must have rolled away! Both these dogs got good forever homes.

Hilda and Philip

Throughout their 53 years of married life, Hilda and Philip have always owned dogs; Collies, Scottish Terriers and Dachshunds, sometimes three at a time. One particularly disorderly rescue Scottie called Jock Mackay required what they called 'intense training' to convert him into their lovely loyal pal. They are always willing to stand in supermarket entrances and the draughty

One of the 'toys' Graham has made for the feral cats.

Victorian Market collecting money for MAA. They say they are humbled by the generosity of Highland folk. Every year, they run a stall at the fete selling all manner of bric-a-brac, books, jigsaws and things that even Hilda finds difficult to attribute to a particular purpose, but she usually manages to sell them! People are unlikely to forget Hilda's entrance to the fete the year she was carried in 'fireman style' over Graham's shoulder. This lovely couple are lifelong animal lovers and staunch supporters of MAA.

Wendy
Wendy took early retirement from a career in health care and moved to the Highlands. She had been walking dogs from two rescue kennels in England and had a passion for big dogs, having four of her own. She was fit and strong so was able to manage all shapes and sizes when she came to MAA eleven years ago. However, a genetic bone disorder kicked in of late and she began to realise she no longer had the strength in her shoulders or hips. The message was rammed home when a particularly large GSD

with a passion for water took her through a bramble patch into a stinking bog, where he wallowed until he was ready to leave, shaking water and muck off his fur onto Wendy, then return himself and her to the kennels! One of the kennel staff enquired if the pair had enjoyed a wee holiday in Thurso since they had been gone so long? Since then, she takes the smaller, older or disabled dogs for walks or those she describes as sensible creatures that look at her and think, "Oh dear, I've got this one to walk today - better go steady!" She still looks longingly at the big dogs but needs must!

Wendy says: "Even if I can only walk one or two dogs that morning, I know I have made a difference to their lives that day. I love the sight, sound, smell and touch of dogs and, fortunately, they usually love me too!"

Sue

Sue is a 1:1 carer for her disabled daughter. It became more difficult for her to find time to get outside in the fresh air and to keep fit because she needed someone to care for her daughter. Although they had always had dogs in the past, her circumstances meant that she could not guarantee a decent quality of life for another one. Sue says that, in common with a lot of long-term carers who end up on the periphery of society and socially isolated, she lacked confidence so she did not approach MAA to ask if she could help. And then she heard a talk from me about MAA and plucked up the courage to call in and offer her services. So, five years ago, Sue started walking wee terriers and Staffies selected by the staff and then progressed to bigger and stronger dogs. It took a while for her to become accustomed to the different behaviours of the dogs, some of whom were unused to interacting with humans or who had been poorly trained and become unmanageable in their homes.

Dog walking at MAA is a wonderful confidence-builder and she was soon putting dogs back in their pens after their walk and putting a lead on the next dog with minimal assistance from kennel staff. Sue walks three mornings a week, regardless of the weather, since she just loves being outdoors surrounded by nature. Equally enjoyable is the craic in the kitchen over a mug of tea and packet of crisps. She talks about the real sense of achievement found in gradually gaining the trust of a frightened and timid dog or gently instilling some acceptable social behaviour in a badly trained dog. Sue developed special relationships with two of our bigger dogs and describes below, in her own words, her experience with Chopper and Bear.

"Both Chopper and Bear pulled on their leads all the way round the wood, usefully adding an upper body work-out to the walk. It is possible to cover a fair mileage during the week and the endorphins produced through walking certainly lift my mood, enabling me to cope better with caring and all the professional services which accompany the role. At the beginning, Chopper threw himself around the pen, chewing his lead when not barking loudly and generally causing chaos. He gradually learned to walk on his lead, but other walkers still had to give him a wide berth since he was still trying to fight with the other dogs. One wet morning, Chopper was towing me round the wood as usual, when my foot slipped on a wet tree root. I was aware that Chopper would be frightened and possibly aggressive and that he might attack me, or at least my face, as I hurtled full length towards the ground. However, opening my eyes seconds later I discovered that I was lying on the moss at the side of the track with Chopper licking my face and wagging his tail fit to burst! From then on we became the best of friends, although he still pulled me round the wood.

"One spring morning Chopper and I were at the top of the wood on the way back to the kennel, when he suddenly stopped dead, sat down beside me and rested his head on my knee, while staring intently at the path in front of us. I realised that the fir cone on the path was actually a sparrow fledgling and that a parent bird was sitting on the bottom branch of hemlock-spruce, desperately calling the baby bird to safety. I would have expected Chopper to have swallowed the fledgling without breaking stride, but here he was, sitting quietly, watching the sparrows intently, without moving a muscle. Eventually the adult bird landed on the path and enticed her fledgling back into the undergrowth, whereupon Chopper stood up and continued on his way back to the kennel.

"Bear was also a larger breed, who also towed me round the wood, not yet having learned to walk on the lead either. He was a dog who did not react at all when I talked to him and was also aggressive with other dogs. One morning he suddenly stood still, staring high into a Scots pine and I realised that he had spotted two young red squirrels chasing each other round the trunk. Suddenly, he bounded from the ground and launched himself at the tree trunk, pushing upwards with his back legs until his bottom was above my head, while the squirrels jumped to another tree trunk, chittering crossly.

"Realising that Bear had run out of steam and was about to fall off the tree trunk, I ran forward hoping to catch him, while realising that he may well be frightened enough to bite me, and also that he would really hurt himself if he landed on his back. However, he dropped gracefully and softly into my out stretched arms and remained completely still, while avoiding eye contact as I turned him over and lowered him gently to the ground. Immediately he set off at speed, towing me along the path and road back to the kennel, periodically looking round with eye contact, as if to say 'Please don't say anything, don't tell anyone, please.' I am afraid that I did tell everyone over a mug of tea in the kennel kitchen, never having met a tree-climbing dog before. Needless to say, we did not see another squirrel in the woods in the following months, but Bear became much more affectionate and really quite cuddly, which I am sure helped him to find his new family and home."

Ollie Owl knew a good thing when he landed on his talons in MAA.

Acknowledgements

My deepest gratitude to all the many people and animals who have been part of the story of Munlochy Animal Aid and without whom there would be no story to turn into a book. My thanks to my friend Wendy Nganasurian for her encouragement and help throughout the writing of this book and to Russell Turner of Bassman Books for his generosity in helping us achieve the end product.